T0215417

Blockchain for Big Data

Blockchain for Big Data
AI, IoT and Cloud Perspectives

Shaoliang Peng

CRC Press
Taylor & Francis Group
Boca Raton London New York

CRC Press is an imprint of the
Taylor & Francis Group, an **informa** business

First edition published 2022
by CRC Press
6000 Broken Sound Parkway NW, Suite 300, Boca Raton, FL 33487-2742

and by CRC Press
2 Park Square, Milton Park, Abingdon, Oxon, OX14 4RN

Library of Congress Cataloging-in-Publication Data
Names: Peng, Shaoliang, 1979- author.
Title: Blockchain for big data : AI, IoT and cloud perspectives / Shaoliang Peng.
Description: First edition | Boca Raton : CRC Press, 2022. | Includes bibliographical references. | Summary: "In this work, the author investigates the researches and applications of blockchain technology in the field of Big Data and assesses the advantages and challenges that blockchain technology may bring to big data. The author also analyses possible future directions of the convergence of blockchain and big data"— Provided by publisher. |
Identifiers: LCCN 2021010668 (print) | LCCN 2021010669 (ebook) |
ISBN 9781032063041 (hbk) | ISBN 9781032063133 (pbk) | ISBN 9781003201670 (ebk)
Subjects: LCSH: Blockchains (Databases)
Classification: LCC QA76.9.B56 P46 2022 (print) | LCC QA76.9.B56 (ebook) | DDC 005.74—dc23
LC record available at https://lccn.loc.gov/2021010668
LC ebook record available at https://lccn.loc.gov/2021010669

ISBN: 978-1-032-06304-1 (hbk)
ISBN: 978-1-032-06313-3 (pbk)
ISBN: 978-1-003-20167-0 (ebk)

Typeset in Minion
by codeMantra

Contents

Preface: Background and Overview

A S AN IMPORTANT RESOURCE, DATA HAS RECEIVED INCREASING attention. In the process of data resource development and utilisation, sharing is always a difficult problem: the government is restrained and worried about leaking secrets; individuals also have concerns and fear that their privacy will be exposed; companies are even tightly shutting the gates. However, modern trade has greatly promoted global production and consumption and promoted the rapid development of the economy and society. Data also needs to flow to reflect value and play a role. Data without circulation has little impact – effectively just a bunch of numbers. Just as the driving force of economic activity is value realisation, as equally valuable data, it needs to have an equivalent value flow in the flow process. This is exactly what the traditional big data industry tends to overlook, and it has also prevented the big data industry from developing well. The blockchain with the digital cryptocurrency gene is born for value and has the ability to make up for the shortboard of big data value circulation. Only big data that fully realises value can truly have a future!

1 THE ADVENT OF THE BIG DATA ECONOMY

In the era of big data, all walks of life are actively using data thinking to transform and innovate. The production model, delivery method, life experience, and management decision-making capabilities of the entire society are evolving to "data socialisation". Data can be used equally by all levels of society, breaking physical boundaries, and permeating every corner of social life. In turn, it drives the realisation of ecological interaction between the virtual world and the real society, so that social resources can be reintegrated, shared, and used on the same platform and ultimately realise all social application values.

Therefore, the new economic model in the future will centre on the information economy, knowledge economy, and smart economy. All of these need to be based on socialised big data, fully integrated and sublimate to conditions, and operated on the commercialisation of big data resources. And paid use as a sign. Only by making big data an effective resource, guided by economic laws and serving the economy and society, can the full use of big data at a higher level be truly realised and the foundation of a data society can be truly laid.

The most attractive part of big data lies in the "data externality", that is, the same set of data can produce different values and utility in different dimensions, and it will also exert different utilities to different users. Therefore, as the dimensions of use increase, the energy and value of data will be magnified. At the same time, data can be "replicated" at a very low marginal cost, which is inherently surplus, so it can be reused to a greater extent across time and space, thereby forming greater social utility.

In the Internet age, the most famous network effect evaluation method is Metcalfe's law. The law states that the value of an Internet is proportional to the square of the number of nodes, and a key assumption is that the relationship between these nodes is of equal value. This law has also become the cornerstone of the Internet economy.

So, what is the cornerstone of the data economy? Data circulation can bring great value. The data circulation here includes not only the transaction and exchange of data but also the openness and sharing of data. The smooth flow of data will effectively lower the threshold for innovation, drive the development of emerging industries, such as the mobile Internet, big data, and data services, and become the engine of the data economy. In the context of the rise of big data as a national strategy, the development of data circulation has even more opportunities for market and policy.

2 BLOCKCHAIN TECHNOLOGY PROMOTING VALUE INTERCONNECTION

In the past few years, blockchain may be the most important development in the IT field. It has the potential to change the way the world approaches big data and enhance security and data quality. For example, on a blockchain supply chain financial service platform, central enterprises, suppliers, and banks are all involved. Central enterprises and financial institutions can intuitively observe various real-time business data of suppliers through the system to provide a basis for future market forecasts.

Furthermore, with the development of business, a large number of data increases. If combined with big data technology, the system will be given huge computing and analysis capabilities. At this time, central enterprises, banks, etc. can directly gain insight into market trends through data. The possible changes brought by the combination of blockchain and big data are as follows: improve data quality through the structured collection of data; improve data security through distributed networks; protect data privacy and simplify data access through cryptography; and algorithm verification to prevent fraudulent activities and achieve reliable real-time data insights.

From the current development of blockchain and big data, we are likely to see further development in this field. As the blockchain technology matures, we may see its innovations in various industries and innovations in business models.

3 OVERVIEW OF THE BOOK STRUCTURE

The book consists of seven parts:

This Preface introduces the background and the structure of the book, including the current state of the big data economy and the value interconnectedness of blockchain technology.

Chapter 1 presents big data technology, including the history of big data and the key technologies of big data.

Chapter 2 provides an introduction and interpretation of blockchain technology, starting with Bitcoin, including some basic concepts of blockchain technology as well as the history of its development and key technologies.

Chapter 3 talks about the symbiotic evolution of the two technologies, big data and blockchain, and how the two technologies intersect and develop. It also explains the similarities and differences between the two technologies.

Chapter 4 focuses on some of the advantages and possible challenges of combining blockchain technology and big data technology.

Chapter 5 addresses some possible application scenarios of the two technologies in real life and some scenarios that have already been grounded.

In Chapter 6, we discuss the possible future direction of the combination of the two technologies.

Author

**Prof. Shaoliang Peng** is the executive director/professor of College of Computer Science and Electronic Engineering/the National Supercomputing Center in Changsha (Hunan University, Changsha, China), and is an adjunct professor of State Key Laboratory of Chemo/Biosensing and Chemometrics, and Peng Cheng Lab. He was a visiting scholar at CS Department of City University of Hong Kong (CityU) from 2007 to 2008 and at BGI Hong Kong from 2013 to 2014. His research interests are high performance computing, bioinformatics, big data, AI, and blockchain. He has published dozens of academic papers on several internationally influential journals, including *Science, Nature Machine Intelligence, Cell AJHG, NAR, Genome Research, ACM / IEEE Transactions, BIBM* and so on, which have been cited by Google Scholar for over 9200 times. He has served as editors of several international journals, including Executive Editors of *International Journal of Biological Sciences* (IJBS), Executive Editors-in-Chief of *Interdisciplinary Sciences: Computational Life Sciences International Journal* (ISCLS), Editors-in-Chief of *Metaverse*, etc. He has also served as chairman and sponsor of the Hunan Provincial Bioinformatics Society, deputy director of biological information professional group in CCF, and Program Chairman of the 17th APBC Asia Pacific Regional Bioinformatics Conference Committee 2019, and BIBM 2016 Conference Invited Speaker.

Acknowledgments

THIS WORK WAS SUPPORTED by NSFC-FDCT Grants 62361166662; National Key R&D Program of China 2023YFC3503400, 2022YFC3400400; The Innovative Research Group Project of Hunan Province 2024JJ1002; Key R&D Program of Hunan Province 2023GK2004, 2023SK2059, 2023SK2060; Top 10 Technical Key Project in Hunan Province 2023GK1010; Key Technologies R&D Program of Guangdong Province (2023B1111030004 to FFH). The Funds of State Key Laboratory of Chemo/Biosensing and Chemometrics, the National Supercomputing Center in Changsha (http://nscc.hnu.edu.cn/), and Peng Cheng Lab.

CHAPTER 1

The Development of Big Data

1.1 THE CONCEPT OF BIG DATA

Gartner defines big data as a massive, high growth rate, and diversified information asset that requires new processing mode to have stronger decision-making power, insight and discovery ability, and process optimisation ability (Ward & Barker, 2013).

McKinsey's definition: big data refers to the data collection that cannot be collected, stored, managed, and analysed by traditional database software tools within a certain period.

Modern society is an information-based and digital society. With the rapid development of the Internet, Internet of Things, and cloud computing technology, data is flooding the whole world, which makes data become a new resource. People must make rational, efficient, and full use of it. The number of data is increasing exponentially, and the structure of data is becoming increasingly complex, which makes 'big data' have different deep connotations from ordinary 'data'.

The volume of data in such fields as astronomy, high-energy physics, biology, computer simulation, Internet applications, and e-commerce has shown a rapid growth trend. According to the United States Internet Data Center (IDC), data on the Internet grows by more than 50% per year, doubling every two years, and more than 90% of the world's data has been generated in recent years. Data does not simply refer to the information that people publish on the Internet; the world's industrial equipment, cars, meters with countless sensors, measuring and transmitting information about position, movement, vibration, temperature, humidity, and even changes in the air quality at any time, also generated a huge amount of data.

Dr. Jim Gray, a famous database expert, author of transaction processing, and Turing Award winner, summed up that in the history of human scientific research, there have been three paradigms, namely, Empirical, Theoretical, and Computational. Today, with the increasing amount of data and the complexity of data structure, these three paradigms can no longer meet the needs of scientific research in new fields, so Dr. Jim Gray proposed the fourth paradigm, a new data research method, namely Data Exploration, to guide and update scientific research in different fields.

The size of data is not the only indicator to judge big data. The characteristics of big data can be summarised in 4Vs, which are volume, velocity, variety, and value.

1.1.1 Large Amount of Data

As we enter the information society, data grows naturally, and its production is not transferred according to human will. From 1986 to 2010, the amount of global data has increased 100 times. In the future, the growth rate of data will be faster. We are living in an era of 'data explosion'. Today, only 25% of the world's devices are connected to the Internet, and about 80% of Internet devices are computers and mobile phones. In the near future, more users will become Internet users, and various devices such as automobiles, televisions, household appliances, and manufacturing equipment will also be connected to the Internet. With the rapid development of Web 2.0 and mobile Internet, people can publish all kinds of information, including blogs, microblogs, WeChat, and so on, anytime, anywhere, and at will. In the future, with the promotion and popularisation of the Internet of Things, all kinds of sensors and cameras will be everywhere in our work and life. These devices automatically generate a large amount of data every moment.

1.1.2 Variety of Data Types

Big data comes from many sources, with new data being generated continuously from scientific research, enterprise applications, and web applications. Biological big data, transportation big data, medical big data, telecom big data, electric power big data, financial big data, etc. are showing a 'blowout' growth, involving a huge number, which has jumped from the TB level to PB level.

The data types of big data are rich, including structured data and unstructured data. The former accounts for about 10%, mainly refer to the data stored in the relational database; the latter accounts for about 90% with various types, mainly including email, audio, video, WeChat, microblog, location information, link information, mobile phone call information, and network log.

Such a wide variety of heterogeneous data brings new challenges and opportunities to data processing and analysis technology.

1.1.3 Fast Processing Speed

In the era of big data, the speed of data generation is very fast. In Web 2.0 applications, Sina can generate 20,000 microblogs, Twitter can generate 100,000 tweets, Apple can download 47,000 applications, Taobao can sell 60,000 products, Renren can generate 300,000 visits, and Baidu can generate 1,000,000 tweets in 1 minute. Facebook generates 6 million page views for 900,000 search queries. The famous Large Hadron Collider (LHC) generates about 600 million collisions per second, generating about 700 MB of data per second, with thousands of computers analysing these collisions.

Many applications in the era of big data need to provide real-time analysis results based on rapidly generated data to guide production and a life practice. As a result, the speed of data processing and analysis is usually in the order of seconds, which is fundamentally different from traditional data mining techniques, which do not require real-time analysis results.

1.1.4 Low-Value Density

As beautiful as it may look, big data has a much lower value density than what is already available in traditional relational databases. In the era of big data, much of the valuable information is scattered throughout the mass of data. In the case of an accident, only a small piece of video recording of the event will be valuable. However, in order to get the valuable video in case of theft, we have to invest a lot of money to buy surveillance equipment, network equipment, storage devices, and consume a lot of power and storage space to save the continuous monitoring data from the cameras.

1.2 THE PAST AND PRESENT OF BIG DATA

At the symposium of the 11th International Joint Conference on Artificial Intelligence held in Detroit, Michigan, USA in 1989, the concept of 'Knowledge Discovery (KDD) in Database' was put forward for the first time. In 1995, the first International Conference on Knowledge Discovery and Data Mining was held. With the increase of participants, the KDD International Conference was developed into an annual meeting. The fourth International Conference on Knowledge Discovery and Data Mining was held in New York in 1998, where not only academic discussions were held but also more than 30 software companies demonstrated their products. For example, Intelligent Miner, developed by IBM, is used to provide a solution for data mining. SPSS Co., Ltd. developed data mining software Clementine based on decision tree. Darwin data mining suite is developed by Oracle, Enterprise of SAS and Mine set of SGI, and so on.

In the academic community, nature launched a special issue of 'big data' as early as 2008, which focuses on the research of big data from the aspects of Internet technology, supercomputing, and other aspects.

Economic interests have become the main driving force, and multinational giants such as IBM, Oracle, Microsoft, Google, Amazon, Facebook, Teradata, EMC, HP, and other multinational giants have become more competitive due to the development of big data technology. In 2009 alone, Google contributed $54 billion to the U.S. economy through big data business; since 2005, IBM has invested $16 billion in more than 30 big data-related acquisitions, making the performance stable and promoting rapid growth. In 2012, the share price of IBM broke the $200 mark, tripled in three years; eBay accurately calculated the return of each keyword in advertising through data mining. Since 2007, advertising expenses have decreased by 99%, while the percentage of top sellers in total sales has increased to 32%; in 2011, Facebook made public, for the first time, a new data processing and analysis platform, Puma. Through the differentiation and optimisation of multiple data processing links, the data analysis cycle is reduced from 2 days to less than 10 seconds, tens of thousands of times more efficient, and large-scale commercial applications based on it have been blooming since then (Wei-Pang & Ntafos, 1992).

In March 2012, the Obama administration announced the 'Big Data Research and Development Initiative', which aims to improve people's ability to acquire knowledge from massive and complex data and develop the core technologies needed for collecting, storing, retaining, managing, analysing, and sharing massive data. Big data has become the focus of information technology after an integrated circuit and the Internet.

People have never stopped to analyse data mining, but the rise of the concept of big data has happened in recent decades. The reason for its formation is the result of the joint action of various factors. If any of the factors is not developed enough, it will not form the hot and extensive application of big data.

1.3 TECHNICAL SUPPORT OF BIG DATA

Information technology needs to solve the three core problems of information storage, information transmission, and information processing, and the continuous progress of human society in the field of information technology provides technical support for the advent of the big data era.

1.3.1 Storage Device Capacity Is Increasing

In recent years, computer hardware technology has developed rapidly, but on the other hand, information and data are also growing. To meet the requirements of information storage, hardware storage devices have been constantly improved. Nowadays, storage cards of the size of fingernails have several gigabytes or even tens of gigabytes of information capacity, which was unthinkable in the past. Hardware storage devices include hard disk, optical disk, U disk, mobile storage device, and so on. This kind of storage devices is collectively referred to as solid-state storage devices. At present, solid-state storage devices are used to store data and information in the world. This is mainly because of its low-carbon manufacturing nature. Besides, it is made of solid-state electronic storage chips through matrix arrangement, which has many advantages. Traditional devices do not have the advantages, so solid-state storage devices become the mainstream storage devices.

In 1956, IBM produced the world's first commercial hard disk with a capacity of only 5 MB. It was not only expensive but also the size of a refrigerator. In 1971, Seagate founder Alan Shugart launched an 8-inch floppy disk storage device, which was no longer so huge. However, at the earliest time, its capacity was only 81 kb. A long document may need several floppy disks to copy. Then, there were 5.25-inch and 3.5-inch floppy disks, and the capacity was no more than 2 MB. In 1973, American Jim

Russell built the first compact disc recording prototype. Since then, CD storage has entered the stage of history. Different storage technologies such as CD, MD, VCD, DVD, and HD-DVD have been developed. The storage capacity has also entered the G era from the M era. From storage cost, HP's tape can store up to 15 TB in a single disk, and the price is only about 900 yuan ($139.88 USD), only 60 yuan ($9.33 USD) per TB. The cheap and high-performance hard disk storage device not only provides a large amount of storage space but also greatly reduces the cost of data storage.

Data volume and storage device capacity complement and promote each other. On the one hand, with the continuous generation of data, the amount of data to be stored is increasing, which puts forward higher requirements for the capacity of storage devices, which urges storage device manufacturers to manufacture products with a larger capacity to meet the market demand; on the other hand, storage devices with larger capacity further speed up the growth of data volume. In the era of high storage equipment prices, due to the consideration of cost issues, some unnecessary devices that cannot clearly reflect the value of data are often discarded. However, with the continuous reduction of the price of unit storage space, people tend to save more data in order to use more advanced data analysis tools to excavate value from it at some time in the future.

1.3.2 Increasing Network Bandwidth

In the 1950s, communication researchers recognised the need to allow conventional communication between different computer users and communication networks. This leads to the study of decentralised networks, queuing theory, and packet switching. In 1960, ARPANET, created by the Advanced Research Projects Agency (ARPA) of the U.S. Department of Defense, triggered technological progress and made it the centre of Internet development. In 1986, NSFNET, a backbone network based on TCP/IP technology, was established by the National Science Foundation of the United States to interconnect the Supercomputer Centre and academic institutions. The speed of NSFNET increased from 56 kbit/s to T1 (1.5 mbit/s) and finally to T3 (45 mbit/s).

The development of Internet access technology is very rapid. The bandwidth has developed from the initial 14.4 kbps to the current 100 Mbps or even 1 Gbps bandwidth. The access mode has also developed from the single telephone dial-up mode in the past to the diversified wired and wireless access methods. The access terminal also begins to develop towards mobile devices.

In the era of big data, information transmission is no longer encountering bottlenecks and constraints in the early stage of network development.

1.3.3 CPU Processing Capacity Increased Significantly

In 1971, Intel released its first 4-bit microprocessor, the 4004 microprocessor, which had a maximum frequency of only 108 kHz. Soon after, Intel introduced 8008 microprocessors, and in 1974, 8008 developed into 8080 microprocessors, thus CPU entered the second generation of microprocessors. The second-generation microprocessors all adopt NMOS technology. Only four years later, 8086 microprocessor was born. It is the first 16-bit microprocessor in the world and the starting point of the third generation microprocessor. In 2000, Pentium 4 was born, when the CPU frequency has reached the GHz level, in 2004 Intel built the 3.4 GHz processor. But the process of CPU is only 90 nm, the consequence of ultra-high frequency is huge heat generation and power consumption, the power of 3.4 GHz CPU can exceed 100 W, and the power consumption of 4 GHz CPU which Intel was developing at that time is unimaginable. The new generation of Pentium 4 chips has not been well received in the market. Intel decided to change from 'high frequency' to 'multi-core' and started the research and development of dual-core, 4-core and 6-core, through multi-core 'human-sea tactics' to improve the efficiency of CPU. More than 10 years later, the manufacturing technology of CPU is also improving, and the main frequency is gradually increasing again. For example, the Core i7 processor of the eighth generation 14 nm achieves the main frequency of 3.7 GHz (turbo frequency 4.7 GHz) and also adopts a 6-core architecture.

The continuous improvement of CPU processing speed is also an important factor in increasing the amount of data. The continuous improvement of the performance of the CPU greatly improves the ability to process data, so that we can deal with the continuous accumulation of massive data faster.

1.3.4 The Deepening of Machine Learning

In the 1980s, the semiotics school was popular, and the dominant method was knowledge engineering. Experts in a certain field made a machine that could play a certain role in decision-making in a specific field, that is, the so-called 'expert machine'.

Since the 1990s, the Bayesian school developed probability theory which became the mainstream thought at that time, because this method with extended attributes can be applied to more scenarios.

Since the end of the last century, the connection school has set off an upsurge, and the methods of neuroscience and probability theory have been widely used. Neural networks can recognise images and speech more accurately and do well in machine translation and emotional analysis. At the same time, because neural networks require a lot of computing, the infrastructure has been a large-scale data centre or cloud since the 1980s.

In the first decade of the 21st century, the most significant combination is that of the connecting school and the semiotics school, resulting in the formation of memory neural networks and agents capable of simple reasoning based on knowledge. Infrastructure is also moving towards large-scale cloud computing.

The in-depth study of machine learning algorithm improves people's ability to process data and can mine rich valuable information from the data.

1.4 THE VALUE OF BIG DATA

The main value system of big data is that it can discover new things beyond our cognition through a large amount of data, which can be embodied in the following aspects.

1.4.1 Big Data Decision-Making Has Become a New Decision-Making Method

Making decisions based on data is not unique to the era of big data. Since the 1990s, data warehouse and business intelligence tools have been widely used in enterprise decision-making. Today, data warehouse has been an integrated information storage warehouse, which not only has the capacity of batch and periodic data loading but also has the ability of real-time detection, dissemination, and loading of data changes. It can also realise query analysis and automatic rule triggering combined with historical data and real-time data, so as to provide strategic decisions (such as macro decision-making and long-term planning) and tactical decision-making (such as real-time marketing and personalised service). However, data warehouse is based on relational database, so there are great limitations in data type and data volume (Maniar & Khatri, 2014). Now, big data decision-making can face a wide range of types of unstructured massive data for decision-making analysis, which has become a new popular decision-making method (Yan, Chen, & Huang, 2016). For example, government departments can integrate big data technology into 'public opinion analysis'. Through the comprehensive analysis of various sources of data such as forum, microblog, WeChat, and community, we can clarify or test the essential facts and trends in the information, reveal the hidden information content contained in the information, make intelligence prediction for the development of things, help realise government decision-making, and effectively respond to various emergencies.

1.4.2 Big Data Application Promotes Deep Integration of Information Technology and Various Industries

Some experts pointed out that big data will change the business functions of almost every industry in the next 10 years. In the Internet, banking, insurance, transportation, materials, energy, services and other industries, the accumulation of big data will accelerate the deep integration of these industries and information technology and open up new directions for industry development. For example, big data can help express delivery companies choose the best travel route with the lowest freight cost, assist investors to choose the stock portfolio with maximum revenue, assist retailers to effectively locate target customer groups, help Internet companies achieve accurate advertising (Mohanty, Jagadeesh, & Srivatsa, 2013), and enable power companies to make distribution plans to ensure grid security. In short, big data has touched every corner, which will lead to great and profound changes in our lives.

1.4.3 Big Data Development Promotes the Continuous Emergence of New Technologies and Applications

The application demand for big data is the source of big data new technology development. Driven by various application requirements, various breakthrough big data technologies will be proposed and widely used, and the energy of data will also be released. In the near future, applications that rely on human judgement will gradually be replaced by applications based on big data. For example, today's auto insurance companies can only rely on a small amount of owner information to classify customers into simple categories, and give corresponding premium preferential schemes according to the number of car accidents. There is no big difference in which insurance company customers choose. With the emergence of the Internet of Vehicles, 'big data of automobiles' will profoundly change the business model of the automobile insurance industry (Liang, Susilo, & Liu, 2015). If a commercial insurance company can obtain the relevant details of customers' vehicles, and use the mathematical model built in advance to make a more detailed judgement on the customer's accident level, and give a more personalised 'one-to-one' preferential scheme, then there is no doubt that this insurance company will have an obvious market competitive advantage and win the favour of more customers.

1.4.4 Big Data as a Strategic Resource

For the government, big data is considered to be an important source of improving the comprehensive national strength and enhancing the competitiveness of the country.

Therefore, the introduction of various policies and guidelines at the national level to guide enterprises and organisations to develop in accordance with the trend has become a way for governments of various countries to compete (Wang, Yang, Feng, Mi, & Meng, 2014).

The U.S. government released the world's first national big data strategy on March 29, 2012 and the federal big data research and development strategic plan on May 23, 2016, to accelerate the process of big data R & D Action proposed by the U.S. government in 2012. In addition, the 'data pulse' plan of the United Nations, the 'data rights' movement of the United Kingdom, the 'ICT comprehensive strategy for 2020' of Japan, and the big data centre strategy of South Korea are all the planning and deployment of the government at the national level from the strategic level.

All sectors of society have great enthusiasm for big data and believe that the introduction of big data can improve their competitiveness. One of the basic motivations for people to have such value expectations is that people think that through big data processing and analysis, we can have insight into the information intelligence and knowledge insight of customers, friends, products, and channels in all dimensions, so as to provide research clues and technical basis for the design of innovative application mode and business model.

1.5 KEY TECHNOLOGIES OF BIG DATA

No matter how complex the structure of big data processing system is, the technology used is very different, but on the whole, it can be divided into the following several important parts. The structure of big data system is shown in Figure 1.1.

From the general process of data processing, we can see that the key technologies needed in the big data environment are mainly for the storage and operation of massive data. After nearly 40 years of development, the traditional relational database has become mature and still evolving data management and analysis technology. As the language of accessing a relational database, SQL has been standardised, and its function and expression ability have been continuously enhanced. However, it cannot be competent for the analysis of large data under the unprecedented environment of the Internet. The relational data management model pursues a high degree of consistency and correctness of the vertical expansion system. By adding or replacing CPU, memory and hard disk to expand the ability of a single point, it will eventually encounter a 'bottleneck'.

The research on big data mainly comes from big companies that rely on data to obtain business interests. As the world's largest information retrieval company, Google company is at the forefront of big data research. In the face of the explosive increase of Internet information, only improving the server performance cannot meet the needs of business. If we

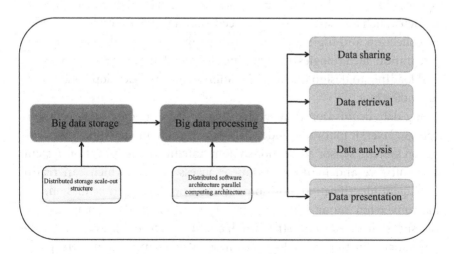

FIGURE 1.1   The structure of big data system.

compare various big data applications to 'cars', the 'highway' supporting the operation of these 'cars' is cloud computing. It is the support of cloud computing technology in data storage, management, and analysis that makes big data useful. Google company expanded from the horizontal, through the use of cheap computer nodes set sample, rewriting software, so that it can be executed in parallel on the cluster, to solve the storage and retrieval function of massive data. In 2006, Google first proposed the concept of cloud computing. The key to support Google's various big data applications is the series of cloud computing technologies and tools developed by Google. Google's three key technologies for big data processing are Google File System (GFS), MapReduce, and BigTable. Google's technical solutions provide a good reference for other companies, and major companies have put forward their own big data processing platform, and the technologies adopted are similar. The key technologies of big data systems will be introduced from the following aspects: distributed file system (DFS), distributed data processing technology, distributed database system, and open-source big data system Hadoop.

1.5.1 Big Data Acquisition Technology

Data collection refers to various types of structured, semi-structured (or weakly structured), and unstructured massive data obtained through RFID radio frequency data, sensor data, social network interaction data, and mobile Internet data. It is the foundation of the big data knowledge service model. The key points are to breakthrough big data collection technologies such as distributed high-speed and high-reliability data crawling or collection and high-speed data full image; to break through big data integration technologies such as high-speed data analysis, conversion, and loading; to design quality evaluation model and develop data quality technology.

Big data acquisition is generally divided into big data intelligent perception layer: it mainly includes data sensing system, network communication system, sensor adaptation system, intelligent identification system, and software and hardware resource access system, which can realise intelligent identification, positioning, tracking, access, transmission, signal conversion, monitoring, preliminary processing, and management of massive structured, semi-structured, and unstructured massive data. We must focus on the technologies of intelligent identification, perception, adaptation, transmission, and access for big data sources. Basic support layer: provide the virtual server required by big data service platform, the database of structured, semi-structured, and unstructured data and Internet of things resources. The key technologies include distributed virtual storage technology, visualisation interface technology for big data acquisition, storage, organisation, analysis and decision-making operation, network transmission and compression technology of big data, and privacy protection technology of big data (Chang et al., 2008).

1.5.2 Big Data Preprocessing Technology

It mainly completes the analysis, extraction, and cleaning of received data.

Extraction: since the acquired data may have multiple structures and types, the data extraction process can help us transform these complex data into a single or easy to process configuration, so as to achieve the purpose of rapid analysis and processing (Chang & Wills 2016).

Cleaning: for big data, not all of them are valuable. Some data are not what we care about, while others are completely wrong interference items. Therefore, we should filter and 'denoise' the data to extract effective data.

1.5.3 Big Data Storage and Management Technology

Big data storage and management should use memory to store the collected data, establish the corresponding database, and manage and call. Focus on complex structured, semi-structured, and unstructured big data management and processing techniques (Chen, Lv, & Song, 2019). It mainly solves several key problems of big data, such as storability, representability, processability, reliability, and effective transmission. Develop reliable DFS, energy efficiency optimised storage, computing into storage, big data's de-redundancy (Dean & Ghemawat, 2004), and efficient and low-cost big data storage technology; breakthrough distributed non-relational big data management and processing technology (Li et al., 2015), heterogeneous data fusion technology, data organisation technology, research big data modelling technology; breakthrough big data index technology; breakthrough big data mobile, backup, replication, and other technologies. Develop big data visualisation technology (Ghemawat, Gobioff, & Leung, 2003).

The database is divided into the relational database, non-relational database, and database cache system. Among them, non-relational database mainly refers to the NoSQL database, which can be divided into key-value database, column storage database, graph database, and document database. Relational database includes traditional relational database system and NewSQL database.

Develop big data security technology. Improve data destruction, transparent encryption and decryption, distributed access control, data audit and other technologies; breakthrough privacy protection and reasoning control (Copeland & Khoshafian, 1985), data authenticity identification and forensics, data holding integrity verification, and other technologies.

1.5.4 Big Data Analysis and Mining Technology

For the development of big data analysis technology, improve the existing data mining and machine learning technology; develop new data mining technologies such as data network mining, special group mining and graph mining; breakthrough big data fusion technologies such as object-based data connection and similarity connection; breakthrough domain-oriented big data mining technologies such as user interest analysis (Dean & Ghemawat, 2004), network behaviour analysis, and emotional semantic analysis.

Data mining is a process of extracting potentially useful information and knowledge from a large number of, incomplete, noisy, fuzzy, and random practical application data. There are many technical methods involved in data mining, including many classification methods (Kumar & Goyal, 2016).

According to the mining task, it can be divided into classification or prediction model discovery, data summary, clustering, association rule discovery, sequential pattern discovery, dependency or dependency model discovery, anomaly, and trend discovery.

According to the mining objects, it can be divided into a relational database, object-oriented database, spatial database, temporal database, text data source, multimedia database, heterogeneous database, heritage database, and global web.

According to the mining method, it can be roughly divided into: machine learning method, statistical method, neural network method, and database method. In machine learning, it can be divided into inductive learning method (decision tree, rule induction, etc.), case-based learning, genetic algorithm, etc. Statistical methods can be subdivided into: regression analysis (multiple regression, autoregression, etc.), discriminant analysis (Bayesian discrimination, Fisher discrimination, nonparametric discrimination, etc.), cluster analysis (systematic clustering, dynamic clustering, etc.), and exploratory analysis (principal component analysis, correlation analysis, etc.). In the neural network method, it can be subdivided into forward neural network (BP algorithm, etc.) and self-organising neural network (self-organising feature mapping, competitive learning, etc.). Database methods are mainly multidimensional data analysis or OLAP and attribute oriented induction (Jun, Yoo, & Choi, 2018).

From the perspective of mining tasks and mining methods, we focus on the breakthrough:

1. Visual analysis. The most basic function for users is to analyse data. Data visualisation can let the data speak by itself and let users feel the results intuitively.

2. Data mining algorithm. Visualisation is to translate machine language to people, and data mining is the mother tongue of the machine. Segmentation, clustering, outlier analysis, and a variety of algorithms allow us to refine data and mine value. These algorithms must be able to cope with the amount of big data but also have a high processing speed.

3. Predictive analysis. Predictive analysis allows analysts to make some forward-looking judgements based on the results of image analysis and data mining.

4. Semantic engine. A semantic engine needs to be designed to have enough artificial intelligence to extract information from data. Language processing technology includes machine translation, sentiment analysis, public opinion analysis, intelligent input, question answering system, and so on.

5. Data quality and data management. Data quality and management is the best practice of management. Data processing through standardised processes and machines can ensure a predetermined quality of analysis results.

1.5.5 Big Data Presentation Technology

Visualisation is one of the most effective ways to explore and understand large data sets. Data are usually boring, relatively speaking, people are more interested in size, graphics, colour, etc. By using the data visualisation platform, the number is placed in the visual space, and the boring data is transformed into rich and vivid visual effects. It will therefore be easier for people to find the hidden patterns, which not only helps to simplify people's analysis process but also greatly improves the efficiency of data analysis.

Data visualisation refers to the process of representing the data in large data sets in the form of graphics and images and discovering the unknown information by using data analysis and development tools. The basic idea of data visualisation technology is to represent each data item in the database as a single graph element, and a large number of data sets constitute the data image. At the same time, each attribute value of the data is expressed in the form of multidimensional data, so that the data can be observed and analysed from different dimensions. Although visualisation is not the most challenging part in the field of data analysis, it is the most important link in the whole data analysis process.

Whether we draw illustrations for demonstration, conduct data analysis, or use data to report news, we are in fact seeking the truth. In some cases, statistics can give false impressions, but it is not the numbers themselves that cause the illusion, but the people who use them. Sometimes it is intentional, but more often it is due to carelessness. If we don't know how to create the right graph, or how to look at the data objectively, we can make a fallacy. However, as long as we master the appropriate visualisation skills and processing methods, we can be more confident in presenting opinions and feel good about our findings (Karafiloski & Mishev, 2017).

1.6 CHAPTER SUMMARY

Big data, as another disruptive technology in the IT industry after cloud computing and Internet of things, attracts people's attention. Big data is everywhere. All walks of life in society, including finance, automobile, retail, catering, telecommunications, energy, government affairs, medical care, sports, and entertainment, are integrated into the imprint of big data. Big data will have a significant and far-reaching impact on human social production and life.

Modern people have many different definitions of big data, among which the four characteristics of big data are very important, namely volume, velocity, variety, and value. From these characteristics, we can see the difference between big data and traditional data mode, so as to grasp big data as a whole and better understand what needs to be paid attention to when big data and blockchain are combined.

It has been several decades since the concept of big data was proposed. There are many excellent technology applications and implementations. The subversive promotion of big data technology to traditional industries has accelerated the development of big data technology. Many enterprises have found that using big data technology can solve the problems that have not been solved in their business field. At the same time, many enterprises have already owned with a large amount of data, we want to realise the value-added of data through big data technology.

The development of big data technology to today's level is closely related to some infrastructure. The capacity of storage equipment is not expanded and the price is decreasing, which makes a large amount of data storage feasible. After accumulating a large amount of data, the demand for big data processing will be generated. The continuous increase of network bandwidth makes information transmission no longer encounter the bottleneck and restriction in the early stage of network development. Enterprises can quickly share a large amount of data, thus increasing the data dimension. Using higher dimensional data can get more information, and at the same time, it also has higher requirements for big data processing capacity. The improvement of processor performance greatly improves the ability of computer to process data, which makes us deal with the massive data accumulated more quickly. Finally, the in-depth study of machine learning algorithm improves people's ability to process data and can mine rich valuable information from the data.

The application of big data corresponds to a series of technologies, including big data acquisition technology, big data preprocessing technology, big data storage and management technology, big data analysis and mining technology, and big data display technology.

REFERENCES

Chang, F., Dean, J., Ghemawat, S., Hsieh, W. C., Wallach, D. A., Burrows, M., ... Gruber, R. E. (2008). Bigtable: A distributed storage system for structured data. *ACM Transactions on Computer Systems, 26*(2), 1–26.

Chang, V., & Wills, G. (2016). A model to compare cloud and non-cloud storage of big data. *Future Generation Computer Systems, 57,* 56–76.

Chen, J., Lv, Z., & Song, H. (2019). Design of personnel big data management system based on blockchain. *Future Generation Computer Systems, 101*(Dec.), 1122–1129.

Copeland, G. P., & Khoshafian, S. N. (1985). A decomposition storage model. *ACM Sigmod International Conference on Management of Data.* https://dl.acm.org/doi/proceedings/. ACM.

Dean, J., & Ghemawat, S. (2004). MapReduce: Simplified data processing on large clusters. *Proceedings of the 6th Conference on Symposium on Operating Systems Design & Implementation - Volume 6.* https://dl.acm.org/conferences. USENIX Association.

Ghemawat, S., Gobioff, H., & Leung, S. T. (2003). The google file system. *ACM Sigops Operating Systems Review, 37*(5), 29–43.

Jun, S. P., Yoo, H. S., & Choi, S. (2018). Ten years of research change using google trends: from the perspective of big data utilizations and applications. *Technological Forecasting and Social Change, 130*(MAY), 69–87.

Karafiloski, E., & Mishev, A. (2017). Blockchain solutions for big data challenges: A literature review. *IEEE EUROCON 2017-17th International Conference on Smart Technologies.* https://ieeexplore.ieee.org/. IEEE.

Kumar, O., & Goyal, A. (2016). Visualization: A novel approach for big data analytics. *Second International Conference on Computational Intelligence & Communication Technology* (pp. 121–124). http://www.proceedings.com/. IEEE.

Li, B., Wang, M., Zhao, Y., Pu, G., Zhu, H., & Song, F. (2015). Modeling and verifying Google file system. *IEEE International Symposium on High Assurance Systems Engineering.* IEEE.

Maniar, K. B., & Khatri, C. B. (2014). Data science: Bigtable, mapreduce and Google file system. *International Journal of Computer Trends and Technology, 16*(3), 115–118.

Mohanty, S., Jagadeesh, M., & Srivatsa, H. (2013). "Big Data" in the Enterprise. *Big Data Imperatives, 8*(2), 23–33.

Liang, K., Susilo, W., & Liu, J (2015). Privacy-preserving ciphertext multi-sharing control for big data storage. *IEEE transactions on information forensics and security, 10*(2), 103–107.

Wang, N., Yang, Y., Feng, L., Mi, Z., & Meng, K. (2014). SVM-based incremental learning algorithm for large-scale data stream in cloud computing. *KSII Transactions on Internet and Information Systems, 8*(10), 3378–3393.

Ward, J. S., & Barker, A. (2013). Undefined by data: A survey of big data definitions. *Computer Science, 3*(8), 220–228.

Wei-Pang, C., & Ntafos, S. (1992). The zookeeper route problem. *Information Sciences, 63*(3), 245–259.

Yan, Y., Chen, C., & Huang, L. (2016). A productive cloud computing platform research for big data analytics. *IEEE International Conference on Cloud Computing Technology & Science, 42*(12), 499–502. https://2020.cloudcom.org/.

CHAPTER 2

Blockchain Technology

2.1 DIGITAL CURRENCY AND BITCOIN

After the advent of the Internet, people began to understand the value of Internet transactions. Digital currency was created under the impetus of this demand. Many digital currencies have emerged, and their implementation methods are different. Some digital currencies are just a flash in the pan, some are only circulating in a small range, some are very popular, but they eventually fail due to various security issues. Only Bitcoin stands out from the numerous digital currencies, surpassing its predecessors and widely circulated in the world. In this section, we will review the development history of digital currency and explore the historical inevitability of the birth of Bitcoin.

2.1.1 Digital Currency

Digital currency belongs to non-physical currency. Non-physical currency is a concept distinguished from physical currency, which refers to the form of money that does not exist in the real world and is not carried by the physical medium, and is divided into electronic currency, virtual currency (narrow), and digital currency. Among them, electronic currency is the electronic 'legal currency'; virtual currency is based on the virtual nature of the network, which is provided by network operators and applied to the network virtual space; digital currency is different from virtual currency, its value is affirmed so that it can be used in real goods and services transactions, not limited to the Internet platform or online games.

Nowadays, the development of cryptocurrency is in a changing boom, but it is not unprecedented. In fact, the first digital currency appeared as early as the 1990s. The original digital currency did not use an encryption mechanism, which is different from the digital cryptocurrency represented by Bitcoin. Therefore, we can divide digital currency into two types: nonencrypted digital currency and digital cryptocurrency.

The first credit cards were born in the early 20th century when large hotels and department stores began to issue paper cards to their high-end consumers. Then, in 1949, Diners Club International, the first company to offer a general merchandise credit card, rose to international fame, while its fees were as high as 7%. Soon in 1958, the Bank of America introduced its first regular credit cards and later the Visa card. Diners Club International is facing strong competition. Until 1966, a series of competitive banks launched MasterCard one after another. In 1990, the birth of the Internet made the concept of digital currency possible. New forms of payment can exist in a purely electronic form, which is beyond people's imagination.

The goal of digital currency is to use money in the digital world just as cash is used in the physical world. The process of using cash in the physical world is that we give our cash to the other person, and then the other party gets the cash and you lose the used cash. But such a thing is not so taken for granted in the digital world. Imagine that in the digital world, we have to pay the other person cash, cash is stored in the form of bytes on your hard drive, you pay yourself to the other person is the same as transferring these bytes of information to someone else, but after the transfer is complete, although the other person received the data representing cash, you do not lose the digital cash, you can continue to use the same digital cash to pay someone else, this is the famous double flower problem. It can be said that the most basic problem to be solved by digital currency is the 'double flower' problem. It was not until the 1990s that a real solution was put into practice, which marked the formal birth of digital currency.

In 1990, David Chaum founded DigiCash, a company in Amsterdam, the Netherlands, to commercialise his research. In 1994, Chaum was invited to give a keynote speech at the first World Wide Web Conference held in Geneva and made a payment from Geneva to Amsterdam through the Internet using DigiCash's software, which was widely reported by media around the world. Chaum has launched two kinds of digital currency systems: ECash and cyberbucks. These two kinds of digital currencies are based on his paper 'blind signatures for untraceable payments' published in 1982, which mentions that the anonymous online payment system using 'blind signature' technology can keep users anonymous and their identities are hard to trace. Although banks can't track how merchants use ECash, they can't be completely anonymous because they will eventually transfer their ECash to the bank. In the end, due to the lack of support and the failure of banks and businesses to adopt the technology properly, it failed. But Chaum's blind signature technology has not disappeared, and it has become an important tool in the implementation of digital currencies.

In 1996, Visa and MasterCard jointly developed the Secure Electronic Transaction (SET) technology, which is a set of digital currency scheme first put forward by people in the industry and implemented, and its core is to realise the payment of assurance, authenticity, and confidentiality.

E-gold digital currency was initiated by Douglas Jackson, a famous oncologist, in 1996. The fact that E-gold lived up to its name and has real gold backing behind it has made it very popular and even had the hope of attracting more than 5 million users in hundreds of countries. Unfortunately, the platform continued to be attacked by hackers and attracted a large number of illegal money laundering transactions, which caused problems for the company in 2009.

Liberty Reserve, another failed digital currency, attempted to create a centralised anonymous remittance platform. The currency allowed users to create accounts and make transfers without any form of authentication. As you might expect, the platform attracted a large number of cybercriminals, leading to its eventual collapse in 2013.

In addition, digital currencies such as Perfect Money and Ven were issued before 2008. They are all nonencrypted digital currencies. In 2008, a landmark invention, Bitcoin, appeared in our field of vision and gradually replaced the past nonencrypted digital currency, occupying the dominant position in the market.

2.1.2 Bitcoin

Bitcoin originated from the paper 'Bitcoin: a peer-to-peer electronic cash system' by Satoshi Nakamoto. In this paper, Nakamoto describes a point-to-point ECash system, which enables all payments to be made directly by both sides of the transaction. It completely breaks away from the traditional payment mode of third-party intermediaries such as commercial banks, thus creating a new monetary system.

Bitcoin was launched in 2009, based on a reference implementation released by Nakamoto and revised by many other programmers. At first, Bitcoin was just an innovation in cryptography, trying to spread among a small group of geeks, and no one was willing to exchange the existing currency with it. After several years of development, Bitcoin has gradually come into public view, and increasingly, businesses began to accept Bitcoin.

The power of the proof of work (PoW) algorithm (mining algorithm), which provides security and reliability for Bitcoin, has increased exponentially and now exceeds the computing power of the world's top supercomputers. Bitcoin has a market value of more than $135 billion. At present, the largest transaction is $400 million, instantly available with just a $1 fee.

Nakamoto stepped out of public view in April 2011, leaving the task of maintaining the Bitcoin code and network to a group of volunteers. The identity of the person or organisation behind Bitcoin is still unknown. However, Nakamoto and others have no control over the Bitcoin system, which is based on fully transparent mathematical principles, open-source code, and consensus among participants. The invention itself is groundbreaking and has produced new science in the fields of distributed computing, economics, and econometrics.

Since 2011, with the establishment of a series of trading markets, the price of Bitcoin began to rise rapidly. As shown in Figure 2.1, by the end

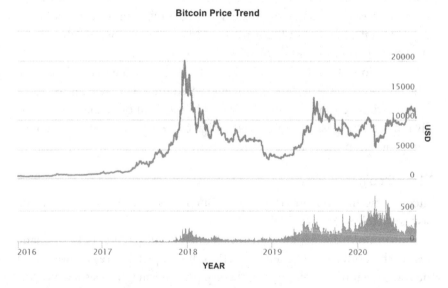

FIGURE 2.1   Bitcoin price trend from 2016 to 2020.

of November 2013, the price of Bitcoin once exceeded $1,000. In the next 2 years, it fell to less than $100 due to the control of various countries. In 2017, its price rose wildly, up to $19,700 high after a rapid decline, and then until now, its price fluctuated around $9,000.

Bitcoin is traded 24 hours a day, and there is no price limit so that its price can fluctuate by thousands of dollars in one day. In this regard, the people's Bank of China and the other five ministries and commissions jointly issued the 'Notice on Prevention of Bitcoin Risk', which does not recognise the monetary attribute of Bitcoin and does not allow it to circulate in the market as a currency. But at the same time, some countries, such as the United States and Germany, hold a relatively optimistic attitude towards Bitcoin and make clear that they are willing to accept Bitcoin. Why do different countries hold different attitudes towards the concept of a salary and thriving currency? The deep-seated reasons behind this are worth discussing.

Bitcoin is a collection of concepts and technologies that make up the digital currency ecology. Bitcoin is also used as a monetary unit to store and transfer value between participants in the Bitcoin network. Bitcoin users mainly use the Bitcoin protocol to communicate through the Internet. Of course, they can also use other transmission networks. Bitcoin stack is open-source, easy to use, and can run on a variety of computing devices, including notebook computers and smartphones.

With Bitcoin, users can do anything traditional money can do, including buying and selling goods, remitting money to people or organisations, or extending credit. Users can buy and sell Bitcoin on special exchanges and exchange them with other currencies. In a sense, Bitcoin is the perfect form of Internet money because it is fast, secure, and borderless.

Unlike traditional currencies, Bitcoin is completely virtual. It has no physical or even digital coins. Bitcoin is implied in the transaction in which the initiator delivers value to the receiver. By owning the key, users can prove ownership of Bitcoin, sign a transaction to unlock the value, and transfer it to the new owner. The key is usually stored in the digital wallet of each user's computer or mobile phone. The key is the only prerequisite for Bitcoin consumption, and the control of Bitcoin is completely in the hands of each user.

Bitcoin is a point-to-point distributed system. There is no central server or control point in the system. Bitcoin is created through a process called mining, in which miners use a lot of computation to guess the answer to a mathematical problem when dealing with Bitcoin transactions. Any participant in the Bitcoin network (the user who runs the full Bitcoin protocol stack on one device) can become miners, using the processing power of their computers to verify and record transactions. On average, every 10 minutes, a miner will work out the answer to a math problem, verify the transactions in the past 10 minutes, and get a new Bitcoin award. In essence, Bitcoin decentralises the central bank's currency issuance and clearing functions, and no central bank is needed.

The Bitcoin protocol contains built-in algorithms for tuning mining methods in the network. The difficulty of the mining process is dynamically adjusted, so no matter how many miners there are in the network, one person will succeed every 10 minutes on average. The total number of Bitcoin is limited to 21 million. Every four years, the issuing rate of Bitcoin will be halved. By 2140, all Bitcoins will be issued. Due to the decreasing speed of Bitcoin issue, Bitcoin is monetary deflation in the long run.

2.2 BLOCKCHAIN

Blockchain is essentially a decentralised database, which is a series of related data blocks generated by cryptography. Each data block contains the transaction information of the whole network for a period of time, which is used to verify the effectiveness of its information (anti-counterfeiting) and generates the next block (Beck, Czepluch, Lollike, & Malone, 2016). Therefore, blockchain is a technical solution to collectively maintain a reliable database in the way of decentralisation and distrust. Generally speaking, blockchain can be called a national accounting technology, or it can be understood as a distributed general ledger technology.

Database is a familiar concept, behind any website or system there is a database, we can think of the database as a ledger. For example, the PayPal database is like a huge account, which records the amount of money in each person's account. When A sends one dollar to B, it is necessary to deduct one dollar from A's account and add one dollar to B's account. The change of this data can be understood as a bookkeeping action. For the general centralised structure, the database behind WeChat is maintained by Tencent's team, while the database behind Taobao is maintained by Alibaba's team. This is a typical centralised database management method, and it is also a matter that everyone thinks is logical. But blockchain completely subverts this approach.

A blockchain system consists of many nodes, which are usually a computer. In this system, each participating node has the opportunity to compete for bookkeeping, that is, to update the database information. The system will select the fastest and best billing node in a period of time (which may be 10 minutes or 1 second) and let it account during this period. It records the changes of data during this period in a data block, which we can think of as a page of paper. After recording the account, the node will send the account book of this page to other nodes. Other nodes will verify whether the account book on this page is correct, and if there is no problem, it will be put into its own account book.

In the system, the data representation of this page of ledger is called block, which records the changes of the whole ledger data during this period. The update result is then sent to every node in the system. As a result, each node of the whole system has exactly the same ledger.

We call this accounting method blockchain technology or distributed general ledger technology.

2.2.1 Blockchain Architecture

From Bitcoin, which first applied the blockchain technology to Ethereum, which first introduced smart contracts to Hyperledger Fabric, which is the most widely used alliance chain, although they are different in their specific implementation, they have many similarities in the overall architecture (Birgit & Ruth, 2018). As shown in Figure 2.2, the blockchain platform can be divided into five layers: data layer, network layer, consensus layer, smart contract layer, and application layer.

2.2.1.1 Data Layer

Bitcoin, Ethereum, and Hyperledger Fabric have their own characteristics in blockchain data structure, data model, and data storage.

In the design of data structure, the existing blockchain platform draws lessons from the research work of Haber and Stornetta, who designed a digital notary service based on document timestamps to prove the creation time of various electronic documents. The timestamp server signs the new document, the current time and the hash pointer pointing to the previous document signature, and the subsequent documents sign the current document signature, In addition, Haber and Stornetta also proposed several schemes, such as grouping multiple documents into blocks, signing for blocks, and organising documents within blocks with Merkle

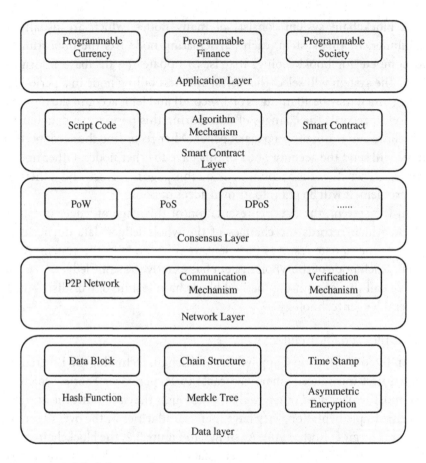

FIGURE 2.2   Blockchain architecture.

tree. Each block in the blockchain consists of block header and block body, which stores batch transaction data, the block header stores Merkle root, previous block hash, timestamp, and other data. The Merkle root generated based on the block transaction data hash realises the unforgeability of block transaction data and simple payment verification; the former block hash generated based on the content of the previous block links the isolated blocks together to form a blockchain; the timestamp indicates the generation time of the block. The block header of Bitcoin also contains data such as difficulty target and nonce to support mining operation in the PoW consensus mechanism.

In the design of the data model, Bitcoin adopts a transaction-based data model. Each transaction is composed of an input indicating the source of the transaction and an output indicating the direction of the transaction. All transactions are linked together through the input and output to make each transaction traceable. Ethereum and Hyperledger Fabric need to support versatile general applications, so the account-based model is adopted, can quickly query the current balance or status based on the account.

In the design of data storage, because blockchain data is similar to the pre-written log of traditional database, it is usually stored in log file format; because the system needs a large number of key-value retrieval based on hash (such as transaction hash-based retrieval of transaction data and block hash-based retrieval of block data), index data and status data are usually stored in key-value database. For example, Bitcoin, Ethereum, and Hyperledger Fabric store index data in level db database.

2.2.1.2 Network Layer

In 2001, Gribble et al. proposed the idea of joint research on the P2P technology and database system. The early P2P database did not have a pre-determined global mode and could not adapt to the network changes and query the complete result set, so it was not suitable for enterprise-level applications. However, the P2P-based blockchain can realise the financial application of digital asset transaction, and there is no central node in the blockchain network, any two nodes can trade directly, and each node can join or exit the network freely at any time. Therefore, the blockchain platform usually chooses the P2P protocol which is completely distributed and can tolerate a single point of failure as the network transmission protocol. The blockchain network nodes have the characteristics of equality, autonomy, and distribution, and all nodes are connected with each other in a flat topology, There is no centralised authoritative node and hierarchical structure. Each node has the functions of route discovery, broadcast transaction, broadcast block, and new node discovery.

The P2P protocol of blockchain network is mainly used to transmit transaction data and block data between nodes. The P2P protocol of Bitcoin and Ethereum is implemented based on the TCP protocol, while the P2P protocol of Hyperledger Fabric is based on the HTTP/2 protocol. In blockchain network, nodes always listen to the broadcast data in the network, and when they receive new transactions and new blocks sent by their neighbours, they will not be able to communicate with each other. It will first verify whether these transactions and blocks are valid, including digital signature in the transaction and workload proof in the block. Only the verified transactions and blocks will be processed (a new transaction is added to the block under construction, and the new block is linked to the blockchain) and forwarded to prevent the continuous spread of invalid data.

2.2.1.3 Consensus Layer

The distributed database mainly uses Paxos and Raft algorithm to solve the problem of distributed consistency. These databases are managed and maintained by a single organisation, and all nodes are trusted. The algorithm only needs to support crash fault tolerance (CFT). Decentralised blockchain is managed and maintained by multiple parties, and its network nodes can be provided by any party, and some nodes may not be trusted. Therefore, it is necessary to support more complex Byzantine Fault Tolerant (BFT). Assuming that there are at most f untrusted nodes in a network with N nodes in total, the Byzantine general problem can be solved under the condition of N≥3F+1 for synchronous and reliable networks.

In order to solve the problem of sybil attack caused by the free access of nodes, the PoW mechanism is applied in Bitcoin. PoW comes from the research work of Dwork and others to prevent spam, that is, only the e-mail that has completed certain calculation work and provided proof will be received. Bitcoin requires that only nodes that have completed a certain amount of computing work and provided proof can generate blocks. Each network node uses its own computing resources to perform hash operation to compete for block bookkeeping rights. As long as the computing resources controlled by trusted nodes in the whole network are higher than 51%, Bitcoin requires that only the nodes that have completed a certain amount of computing work and provide proof can generate blocks. In order to avoid the power consumption caused by high dependence on the computing power of nodes, researchers propose some mechanisms that can reach a consensus without relying on computing power. Peercoin applies the Proof of Stake (PoS) mechanism which is inversely proportional to node ownership; Bitshares uses the Delegated Proof of Stake (DPoS) mechanism which generates blocks alternately according to established periods by several delegates who have voted most by shareholders. Hyperledger Sawtooth applies the Proof of Elapsed Time (PoET) mechanism based on Intel SGX trusted hardware.

The consensus based on the proof mechanism is usually applicable to public chains in which nodes are free to enter and exit, for example, the PoW mechanism is used in Bitcoin and Ethereum. Consensus based on the voting mechanism is generally applicable to alliance chains authorised by nodes, and Hyperledger Fabric uses PBFT algorithms.

2.2.1.4 Smart Contract Layer

Smart contract is a kind of digital protocol that uses algorithms and programs to compile contract terms, deploy on the blockchain, and execute automatically according to the rules. The concept was proposed by Szabo in 1994 and was initially defined as a set of commitments defined in digital form, including the protocols required by contract participants to implement these commitments. The original intention is to build smart contracts into physical entities to create flexible and controllable smart assets. Due to the limitations of early computing conditions and the lack of application scenarios, smart contracts have not been widely concerned by researchers. Until the advent of blockchain technology, smart contracts were redefined. Blockchain realises decentralised storage, and Smart contract realises decentralised computing on the basis of it.

Bitcoin script is a set of instructions embedded in Bitcoin transactions. Due to the single instruction type and limited implementation function, Bitcoin script can only be regarded as the prototype of smart contract. Ethereum provides Turing complete script language Solidity, Serpent and sandbox environment Ethereum Virtual Machine (EVM) for users to write and run smart contracts. Hyperledger Fabric's smart contract is called Chaincode, which selects docker containers as sandbox environments. The Docker container contains a set of signed base disk images and the runtime environment of Go, Java, and SDK, to run Chaincode written in Go or Java languages.

2.2.1.5 Application Layer

The applications on the Bitcoin platform are mainly based on Bitcoin digital currency transactions, while Ethereum platform supports decentralised application (Dapp) in addition to Ethereum-based digital currency transactions. Dapp is a Web front-end application built by JavaScript, which communicates with intelligent contracts running on Ethereum nodes through JSON-RPC. Hyperledger Fabric is mainly oriented to enterprise-level blockchain applications and does not provide digital currency. It can be built based on the SDKs of Go, Java, Python, Node.js, and other languages and communicates with smart contracts running on Hyperledger Fabric nodes via gRPC or REST.

2.2.2 Characteristics of Blockchain

2.2.2.1 No Tampering

The most easily understood feature of blockchain is that it cannot be tampered with.

Tamper-proof is based on the unique ledger of 'block&chain': blocks with transactions are added to the end of the chain in chronological order. To modify the data in a block, you need to regenerate all blocks after it (Chandan, Potdar, & Rosano, 2020).

One of the important functions of the consensus mechanism is that it is almost impossible to modify a large number of blocks because of the high cost. Take the blockchain network (such as Bitcoin and Ethereum) with PoF as an example, only with 51% of the computing power it can regenerate all blocks to tamper with data. However, destroying data is not in the interests of players with large computing power. This practical design enhances the reliability of data on the blockchain.

Generally, the transaction data in the blockchain ledger can be regarded as not 'modified', and it can only be 'corrected' by new transactions recognised. The correction process will leave traces, which is why the blockchain cannot be tampered with.

In the commonly used files and relational data, the system itself does not record the trace of modification unless special design is adopted. The design of blockchain account book is different from that of files and databases. It draws lessons from the design of account books in reality - keeping records. Therefore, we cannot 'modify' the account book without leaving traces but can only 'correct' the account book.

The data storage of blockchain is called 'ledger', which is very consistent with its essence. The logic of the blockchain ledger is similar to that of the traditional ledger. For example, I may have wrongly transferred a sum of money to you, and the transaction is accepted by the blockchain ledger and recorded in it. The way to correct the mistake is not to modify the account book directly and restore it to the state before the wrong transaction; it is to make a new correction transaction, and you will transfer the money back to me. When a new transaction is accepted by the blockchain ledger, the errors and omissions are corrected. All the correction processes are recorded in the account book and can be traced.

The first kind of assumption to put blockchain into use is to take advantage of its non-tamperable characteristics. The application of traceability of agricultural products or commodities is to record their circulation process on the blockchain to ensure that the data records are not tampered with, so as to provide evidence for traceability. One idea of applying blockchain in the field of supply chain is to ensure that people who have access to the account book cannot modify the past records, so as to ensure the reliability of the records.

In March 2018, in the 'White Paper on Blockchain Technology Practices' published by the e-tailing group JD.COM. JD.COM argued that the three application scenarios for blockchain technology (distributed ledger) are: collaboration across entities, the need for low-cost trust, and the existence of long-cycle transaction chains. The multi-agent cooperates on an unalterable account book, which reduces the cost of trust. The status is stored in the blockchain ledger, the state of the data not involved will not change, and the earlier the data, the more difficult it is to tamper with, which makes it suitable for long-term transactions.

2.2.2.2 Uniqueness Required to Express Value

Whether it is an interchangeable pass, a non-interchangeable pass, or some other proposed pass standard, Ethereum's token shows an important feature of the blockchain: the uniqueness required to express value (Gervais, Karame, Wüst, Glykantzis, & Capkun, 2016).

In the digital world, the most basic unit is bit, and the fundamental characteristic of bit is that it can be copied. But value cannot be copied, it must be unique. As we have discussed before, this is the paradox: in the digital world, it is hard to make a single file unique, at least not universally. That is why we now need a centralised ledger to record value.

In the digital world, we can't hold money like we have cash. In the digital world, we need credit agencies like banks, and our money is recorded by bank books.

Digital blockchain technology can bring universal value to the world for the first time.

In early 2018, two leaders of China's technology Internet enterprises coincidentally emphasised the 'uniqueness' brought by blockchain. Ma Huateng, Tencent's chief founder and CEO, said: 'blockchain is indeed an innovative technology. With digital expression of uniqueness, blockchain can simulate the uniqueness of real objects in reality'.

Robin Li, founder and CEO of Baidu, said: 'after the arrival of the blockchain, we can really make the virtual products unique, and the Internet will be very different from the previous Internet'.

The discussion and Prospect of the token economy is based on the fact that in the digital world, blockchain provides a decentralised way of value representation and value transfer on the network basis. In the era of blockchain 2.0 represented by Ethereum, a more general value representative, token, has emerged, from the digital cash period of blockchain 1.0 to the period of digital assets.

2.2.2.3 Smart Contract

From Bitcoin to Ethereum, the biggest change in blockchain is 'smart contract'. Bitcoin system is designed for a digital currency. Its UTXO and script can also handle some complex transactions, but it has great limitations. Vitalik created the Ethereum blockchain, and his core goals are all around smart contracts: a Turing complete scripting language, a virtual machine (EVM) running smart contracts, and a series of standardised smart contracts for different types of certificates.

The emergence of smart contract makes it possible for two people based on blockchain not only to carry out simple value transfer but also to set complex rules to be executed automatically and autonomously by smart contract, which greatly expands the application possibility of blockchain.

At present, the projects that focus on the innovative application of token are realised by writing smart contracts at the software level. With smart contracts, we can trade complex digital assets.

In the Ethereum white paper, Vitalik wrote: Contract should be regarded as 'autonomous agents' existing in the Ethereum execution environment. It has its own Ethereum account, receives transaction information, and they are equivalent to being poked, and then it automatically executes a piece of code (Kosba, Miller, Shi, Wen, & Papamanthou, 2016).

2.2.2.4 Decentralised Self-Organisation

So far, the organisation and operation of major blockchain projects are closely related to this feature. The ideal expectation of many people for blockchain projects are that they become a community or ecology that operates autonomously.

The anonymous Nakamoto disappeared completely from the Internet after completing the development of Bitcoin and the initial iterative development. However, both the Bitcoin protocol, Bitcoin's distributed ledger and decentralised network, Bitcoin miners and Bitcoin development are all self-organised, maintaining this decentralised system (Lemieux, 2016).

We can reasonably speculate that after Bitcoin, there are many competing currencies formed by modifying parameter bifurcation and Bitcoin cash (BCH) formed by hard fork, which may be consistent with Nakamoto's assumption. He chose 'out of control', which can be regarded as a synonym for autonomy.

So far, Ethereum project is still under Vitalik's 'leadership', but as discussed at the beginning of this chapter, he leads the project by leading an open-source organisation, just as Linus leads the open-source Linux operating system and the Linux foundation.

Vitalik may be one of the people who think most about decentralised self-organisation. He has always emphasised and adopted the blockchain-based governance approach. The hard fork of Ethereum in 2016 was proposed by him, but it can be implemented only after it is approved by the community vote on the chain. In Ethereum community, many standards, including ERC20, are formed spontaneously by community developers.

In the book *Decentralized Applications*, the author Siraj Raval also makes a distinction from another perspective, which helps us better understand the application and organisation of the future. He looked at the existing Internet technology products from two dimensions: one is whether it is organisationally centralised or decentralised; the other is whether it is logically centralised or decentralised.

'Bitcoin is organizationally centralized and logically centralized', he says, 'while the e-mail system is decentralized both organizationally and logically'.

When we think about future organisations, the ideal prototype in our minds is often the Bitcoin organisation: a completely decentralised autonomous organisation (Pass, Seeman, & Shelat, 2017). But in the process of practice, in order to promote efficiency, we will slightly move closer to the centralised organisation, and finally, find a suitable balance point.

Now, in the blockchain projects that create and issue passes through the smart contract of Ethereum and run in a community or ecological way, the ideal state of many projects are similar to Bitcoin organisations, but the actual situation is between completely decentralised organisations and traditional companies.

In discussing the fourth feature of the blockchain, decentralised self-organisation, we're actually already moving outward from the world of code, involving human organisation and collaboration. Now, various discussions and practical explorations have also revealed the significance of blockchain beyond technology: it may serve as an infrastructure to support human production organisation and collaborative change. This is another example that blockchain and the Internet are completely isomorphic. Like the Internet, blockchain will be more than just technology and will change the way people organise and collaborate.

Now, many people eagerly trying to enter the blockchain 3.0 stage, that is, they no longer use blockchain for digital asset transactions, but rather they want to apply blockchains to various industries and fields, from the Internet empowerment to blockchain empowerment, from the 'Internet+' to 'blockchain+'. Continue to look forward to the future with the development of the information internet as a contrast. The earliest use of the information internet is to transmit text information, but its real explosion is the subsequent emergence of e-commerce, social networking, games, and O2O, which is combined with offline. In the future, the real display of blockchain value will also be a variety of now-unknown applications.

2.2.3 Classification of Blockchain

According to the degree of openness, blockchain can be divided into public blockchain, consortium blockchain and private blockchain.

2.2.3.1 Public Blockchain: Everyone can Participate

Typical cases: BTC, ETH

Features: the system is the most open, anyone can participate in the maintenance and reading of blockchain data, easy to deploy applications, completely decentralised, and not controlled by any organisation (Paul, Sarkar, & Mukherjee, 2014).

If we take an analogy to reality, the public blockchain maybe like nature or universe in which everyone is in, and no dominant central force is or has yet to be discovered.

At present, when many people are talking about the concept of blockchain, most of them are talking about public blockchain. For example, some people understand that the blockchain is a public database, but obviously, the consortium blockchain and private blockchain are not public databases.

2.2.3.2 Consortium Blockchain: Only Consortium Members can Participate

Typical case: Hyperledger Fabric

Features: the system is semi-open and can only be accessed by registration permission. From the perspective of users, the consortium blockchain is limited to the participation of alliance members, and the scale of alliance can be as large as between countries or between different institutions and enterprises.

By analogy with reality, consortium blockchain is like a variety of chamber of commerce consortium. Only members in the organisation can share interest and resources (Dutta, Choi, Somani, & Butala, 2020). The application of blockchain technology is only to make alliance members trust each other more.

2.2.3.3 Private Blockchain: Only for Individuals or Companies

Typical case: Multichain

Features: the system is the most closed and only used by enterprises, state institutions, or individual individuals (Dinh, Wang, Chen, Liu, & Tan, 2017). It cannot completely solve the trust problem but can improve auditability.

Analogy with reality, the private chain is like a private house, which is generally used by individuals. It's against the law to break into houses without permission. Hacking into a private chain is like hacking into a database.

2.3 CONSENSUS

In the distributed system, consistency (also called agreement in the early days) refers to that for multiple service nodes in the system, given a series of operations, under the protection of protocol (usually through some consensus algorithm), trying to make them reach a certain degree of agreement on the processing results. If the distributed system can achieve 'consistency', it can appear as a 'virtual processing node' with normal function and better performance and stability.

For example, a film company has two ticket offices, both of which sell a certain movie ticket, with a total of 10,000 tickets. So, when a customer arrives at a cinema to buy a ticket, how can the conductor decide whether to sell the ticket or not, so as to avoid overselling? What about when there are more cinemas?

According to the standard, the ideal consistency of distributed system should meet the following requirements:

1. Termination: consistent results can be completed in a limited time;

2. Consensus: the final decision results of different nodes should be the same;

3. Validity: the result of a decision must be a proposal from another process.

In a word, distributed consistency means that all nodes in the system reach the same result on the proposal of a certain node in the system within a certain period of time (Peters & Panayi, 2015). The proposal can be the sequence of multiple events, the value corresponding to a key, the identity of each node in the system, and so on.

And to ensure that the system meets different levels of consistency, it is often necessary to reach through consensus algorithms. At the beginning of the establishment of most distributed systems, such as distributed storage system, the first thing to solve is the problem of consistency. If each node in a distributed system is guaranteed to operate with strong performance (instant response and high throughput) without failures, the implementation of the consensus process is not complicated and can be simply voted on through the multicast process. Unfortunately, such an 'ideal' scenario does not exist in reality. The main points to be considered are the following.

1. The network communication between nodes is unreliable, including arbitrary delay interruption, and content failure;

2. The processing of the node may be wrong, or even the node itself may be down at any time;

3. Synchronous call will make the system not scalable;

4. There are malicious nodes that deliberately want to destroy the system

Generally, failure (non-response) is called 'non-Byzantine error', while malicious response are called 'Byzantine error'. The consistency problem is a classic problem studied since the 1970s. Fischer, Lynch, and Patterson (FLP), three scientists who set the upper limit for consistency problem, proposed FLP impossibility in a paper published in 1985, one of the important theorems of cloth theory. They believe that in a fully asynchronous system, there is no protocol that can tolerate even a process failure and reach an agreement import describing the problem of fault tolerance and consistency in distributed systems and propose the Byzantine general problem for the first time: Byzantine is located in Istanbul, now Turkey. In order to defend the country, the armies are far apart, so the communication between generals must rely on messengers. In order to attack and withdraw uniformly (Radziwill, 2018), an agreement must be reached on actions. But some generals can be traitors who deliberately send misinformation to disturb others. How to form such a storage structure, how to ensure its trustworthiness, how to ensure its security, and how to ensure the consistency of distributed storage all depend on the consensus mechanism. Therefore, the consensus mechanism is the soul of the blockchain, and the working principle and application scenario of the blockchain depend on the consensus mechanism. The goal of blockchain negotiation is to have common nodes form a consistent blockchain structure that needs to meet the following properties: (1) Consistency: all honest nodes keep the prefix part of the blockchain exactly the same and (2) validity: information posted by an honest node will eventually be recorded by all other nodes in its own blockchain.

At present, the common consensus mechanisms are as follows:

2.3.1 Paxos and Raft

In 1990, Lamport's Paxos algorithm maximised the consistency of distributed systems from an engineering perspective. The algorithm classifies nodes into three types. (1) Proposer: the person who submits a proposal for approval, it is usually the role of the customer; (2) accepter: responsible for voting on the proposal, the general role of the server; and (3) learner: be informed of the result of negotiation and unify with it. It can be client or server.

The basic process includes the applicant's recommendation and when more than half of the support is given, the results are sent to all for confirmation. A very small probability is that in each new round of proposals, the proposer crashes and the system will not reach consensus (Saleh, 2018). Therefore, if Paxos can guarantee that the system can reach consensus, there must be more than 1/2 of the normal nodes present.

Raft algorithm is a simplified implementation of the Paxos algorithm, which includes three roles: leader, candidate, and follower, the basic process is: (1) leader election: each candidate will randomly propose an election plan for a certain period of time, and the majority of votes with the latest stage will be elected as the leader. (2) Synchronise logs: the elected leader will find the latest record of the logs in the system and force all of his followers to refresh to that record.

2.3.2 BFT and PBFT

In Byzantine problem (Lamport, Shostak, & Pease, 2019), if the total number of nodes are n and the number of malicious generals are f, when N≥3F+1, the BFT algorithm can be solved. Lamport proves that there is an effective algorithm that can achieve consistent results when the number of honest people is more than 2/3, but it is difficult to ensure consistency if there are too many defectors. PBFT was proposed by Castro and Liskov in 1999. It was the first widely used BFT algorithm. As long as 2/3 nodes in the system work normally, the consistency can be guaranteed. This algorithm consists of three stages: preparation, preparation, and submission. This type of mechanism is characterised by a quick block out and consensus so quickly that there is no time to allow for fork. However, this kind of mechanism requires two nodes to communicate in a closed set of nodes, so it is more suitable for alliance chain and private chain with few nodes. Most alliance chains use mature PBFT mechanisms and its corresponding variants like RAFT, DBFT, and HBFT to reach consensus.

2.3.3 Proof of Work

In the Bitcoin system, new transactions are generated all the time, and the nodes need to put legal transactions into the block. The block header contains six parts, which are version number, previous block hash value, Merkle root, timestamp, difficulty target nonce, and random number (Conti, Kumar, Lal, & Ruj, 2018). Participants need to find random numbers to make the block header hash less than or equal to the difficulty target. For example, the binary representation of a difficult target starts with 32 zeros, and it takes an average of 232 attempts to solve this problem. The difficult target will be adjusted for every 2,016 blocks, with the aim of keeping the average speed of the block out at every 10 minutes, so that the difficulty target will be updated every 2 weeks (2,016×10 minutes). PoW guarantees that transactions that appear in the system for a period of time can be calculated. Until now, the PoW mechanism exists more or less in Dogecoin, Litecoin, and other digital currencies.

2.3.4 PoS

In 2011, on the digital currency enthusiast Bitcointalk forum, the enthusiast named 'QuantumMechanic' proposed the PoS mechanism. After discussion, the community agreed and endorsed. If the PoW competition is computational power, the mining probability is positively correlated with the computational power. The more nodes there are, the greater the probability of mining blocks. The criterion of qualified blocks of PoS can be expressed as f(timestamp)<target×balance. Compared with PoW, the difficulty value in the formula becomes a timestamp, and on the right side of the formula, there is an equilibrium factor. In this way, the overall target value is affected by the equilibrium value and time. Time is limited, so the time out of the block must be within a certain range. Blocks that are too early or too late will not be accepted by other nodes (Wang, Bai, Wang, Liew, & Zhang, 2020). In some cryptocurrency implementations, the balancing factor in the formula is changed to the amount of currency held, resulting in the so-called 'age of the currency'. Due to the limited timestamp, the success rate of PoS forging blocks is mainly related to the equilibrium factor. Unlike the competitive nature of mining, PoS is more like a lottery, accumulating more monetary age for the chance to win, but because once a certain value is consumed, the probability of winning again decreases, avoiding 'the rich getting richer'. In PoS, the main chain is defined as the highest consuming chain and each block transaction will be submitted to increase the score for the block. In this case, the attacker has to have a lot of money to launch an attack on the main chain and accumulate a lot of time in the PoS system, the attacker gets a lot of money and consumes even more. And in the event of an attack or sabotage, the attacker's own funds will be damaged. It may have eliminated the attacker's incentive to act from the beginning, and once the block is created, its age is immediately removed, which will ensure that the attacker cannot continue the attack. After the emergence of the idea of PoS, many protocols based on this secondary development can be considered as PoS system protocols.

2.3.5 PoI

Proof of Importance (PoI) is a fairer algorithm. People don't need to use more powerful machines, and they don't need to hold more stocks to get more returns. It only needs to prove its importance in order to get the block right and get the reward. It doesn't need special mining equipment, it can even run in raspberry pie, so it saves power resources. New Economy Movement (NEM) uses PoI (Mijovic, Miletic, Dimitrijevic, Stojanovic, Zivanovic, & Cuturilo, 2019), where specifically the importance of a node is judged based on the number of wallet interactions and monetary assets.

In contrast, other digital currencies do not take into account the support of nodes for the network. In order to encourage users to actively trade maintenance on the NEM network, it will later include the number of transmissions as a factor of importance.

2.4 THE EVOLUTION OF BLOCKCHAIN TECHNOLOGY

2.4.1 The First Year of Blockchain History

In 1976, Bailey W. Diffie and Martin E. Hellman, two masters of cryptography, published the paper 'New Directions in Cryptography', which covered all the new areas of progress in cryptography for the next few decades, including asymmetric cryptography, elliptic curve algorithms, hashing, and some other means. It not only establishes the development direction of cryptography so far but also plays a decisive role in the technology of blockchain and the birth of Bitcoin.

In the same year, another seemingly unrelated event happened. Hayek published his last economic monograph, 'Denationalization of Money'. The concepts of this monograph, such as non-sovereign currency and competitive currency issuance, have become the core guidelines for the decentralised currency.

Therefore, we can regard 1976 as the first year of the prehistoric era of blockchain, officially opening the whole era of cryptography, including cryptography currency.

Then in 1977, the famous RSA algorithm was born, which should be said to be the natural continuation of the 'New Directions in Cryptography' (Kocher, 1996). It was not surprising that the three inventors won the Turing prize in 2002. However, the patent they applied for RSA was not recognised by many people in the world when it was generally accepted that the algorithm could not be applied for the patent. It was prematurely invalid in 2000.

In 1980, Merkle Ralf proposed the Merkle tree data structure and corresponding algorithm. One of the main uses of Merkle tree was to verify the correctness of data synchronisation in distributed networks, which was also an important means of block synchronisation verification introduced into Bitcoin. It was worth noting that in 1980, the really popular hash algorithm and distributed network did not appear. For example, SHA-1 and MD5, as we know it, were all born in the 1990s. In that era, Merkle released such a data structure, which later played an important role in cryptography and distributed computing, which was somewhat surprising.

In 1982, Lamport proposed the Byzantine General problem, marking a substantial stage in the theory and practice of reliability in distributed computing. In the same year, David Chaum proposed the cryptographic payment system ECash, and it could be seen that with the progress of cryptography, discerning people have begun to try to apply it to money and payment-related fields, and it should be said that ECash was one of the earliest pioneers of cryptographic money.

In 1985, Koblitz and Miller each independently proposed the famous Elliptic Curve Cryptography (ECC) algorithm. Since the previously invented algorithm of RSA was too computationally intensive to be practical, the ECC really made the asymmetric cryptosystem possible. Thus, it can be said that by 1985, about 10 years after the publication of 'New Directions in Cryptography', the theoretical and technical foundations of modern cryptography had been fully established.

It was interesting to note that the period 1985-1997 has not been particularly remarkable in terms of advances in cryptography, distributed networks, and areas related to payment or currency. In my view, this phenomenon is easy to understand: when new ideas, concepts, and technologies are first created, there is always a considerable amount of time for people to learn, explore, and practice before breakthroughs are possible. The first decade tends to be a period of theoretical development, while the second decade moves into the phase of practical exploration, and the decade or so from 1985 to 1997 should be a period of rapid development of the relevant field in terms of practice. Eventually, after about 20 years from 1976, the field of cryptography and distributed computing finally entered an explosive period.

In 1997, The hashcash method, also known as the first generation of PoW algorithm, was invented at that time, which was mainly used for anti-spam. In various papers published subsequently, the specific algorithm design and implementation have completely covered the PoW mechanism used by Bitcoin later.

By 1998, the complete idea of cryptocurrency finally emerged. Wei Dai and Nick Szabo put forward the concept of cryptocurrency at the same time. Among them, Dai Wei's B-money was called the spiritual pioneer of Bitcoin, while Nick Saab's Bitgold outline was very similar to the characteristics listed in Nakamoto's Bitcoin paper so that some people once suspected that Szabo was Nakamoto. Interestingly, it was 10 years since the birth of Bitcoin.

With the advent of the 21st century, there have been several major advances in the field of blockchain. The first is the peer-to-peer distributed network. During the three years from 1999 to 2001, Napster, EDonkey 2000, and BitTorrent appeared successively, laying the foundation for P2P network computing.

Another important event in 2001 was the release of the SHA-2 series of algorithms by the NSA, including the most widely used SHA-256 algorithm, which was the hash algorithm adopted by Bitcoin. It should be noted that by 2001, all the technical foundations for the birth of Bitcoin or blockchain technology were solved in theory and practice, and bitcoin is ready to emerge.

In human history, we often see such a phenomenon, it takes about 30 years for an idea and technology to be put forward and developed (Watanabe, Fujimura, Nakadaira, Miyazaki, Akutsu, & Kishigami, 2016). This phenomenon is not only common in the field of technology but also in other fields such as philosophy, natural sciences, and mathematics, and the creation and development of the blockchain follow this pattern. This model is also easy to understand because it takes a generation for an idea, an algorithm, and a technology to be digested, explored, and practiced.

2.4.2 Blockchain 1.0

This stage is 'one chain one coin'. In this era, every time a digital currency is created, a chain must be created. These digital currencies are created by modifying the parameters of the Bitcoin source code, so the name 'altcoin' or 'copycat coin' also originates from this era. At present, there are still many digital currencies with one currency chain in Initial Coin Offering (ICO). The main problems of one currency one chain are the optimisation of consensus algorithm, hacker attack, and the maintenance of the chain by the core team.

In November 2008, Nakamoto published his famous paper 'Bitcoin: A Peer-to-Peer Electronic Cash System'. In January 2009, Nakamoto used his first version of software mining out the genesis block, including this sentence: 'The Times 03/Jan/2009 Chancellor on brink of second bailout for banks', it opened the era of Bitcoin like a magic spell. There are several important time nodes in the development of Bitcoin.

In September 2010, the first mining site Slush invented a way for multiple nodes to cooperate in mining, which became the beginning of the Bitcoin mining industry. We should know that in May 2010, 10,000 Bitcoin was only worth $25. If calculated according to this price, all Bitcoin (21 million) would be worth $50,000. It is obviously meaningless to concentrate on mining. Therefore, the decision to build a mine pool means that some people believe that Bitcoin will become a virtual currency with unlimited growth space that can be exchanged with real-world currencies in the future. This is undoubtedly a kind of foresight.

In April 2011, the first officially documented (https://bitcoin.org/en/-version-history) version of Bitcoin was released: 0.3.21, a very preliminary, yet significant, version. First of all, because it supports uPNP and realises the ability of P2P software that we use every day, Bitcoin can really enter the house of ordinary people, so that anyone can participate in transactions. Second, before that, the minimum unit of Bitcoin node only supported 0.01 Bitcoin, which was equivalent to 'cent', but this version really supports 'Satoshi'. It can be said that after this version, Bitcoin has become what it is now, and it has really formed a market. Before that, it was basically the plaything of technicians.

In 2013, Bitcoin released version 0.8, the most important version in the history of Bitcoin, which improved the entire internal management of the Bitcoin node itself and optimised network communication. It was only after this point in time that Bitcoin truly supported large-scale transactions across the Internet, became the electronic cash that Satoshi envisioned, and had a truly global impact.

Things are not always so smooth. In the most important version 0.8, Bitcoin introduces a big bug, so after the release of this version, Bitcoin appears hard fork in a short time, resulting in the whole Bitcoin finally having to go back to the old version, which also leads to a sharp drop in the price of Bitcoin.

The development behind Bitcoin is well known by more and more people. For example, the attitudes of countries around the world towards it, the growth of computing power, reaching 1EH/s in January 2016, and more than 10,000 related open-source projects on GitHub prove that the ecological environment of Bitcoin is fully mature.

If you look at the history of Bitcoin from the above perspectives, you may have the same feeling as me: no matter how powerful Nakamoto's curse is and how promising the digital/cryptography currency is, it still depends on the development of software bit by bit. If the software itself has fatal bugs, the whole system will eventually become meaningless.

2.4.3 Blockchain 2.0

Blockchain 2.0 refers to smart contracts. It combined with currency, providing a wider range of applications in the financial sector. Blockchain has strong inherent advantages over financial scenarios. Simply speaking, if banks carry out cross-border transfers, they may need to open various environments, currency exchange, transfer operations, cross-line issues, etc. While the point-to-point operation of blockchains avoids third-party intervention, directly realises transfer, thus improves efficiency.

Smart contract is an early concept, 'A smart contract is a set of digitally defined promises, including an agreement on which the contract participants can execute these promises'.

The blockchain 2.0 is represented by Ethereum. Ethereum is a platform that provides various modules for users to build applications. The applications on top of the platform are in fact smart contracts. This is the core of Ethereum technology. Ethereum provides a powerful programming environment for contracts, which enable complex logic in both commercial and non-commercial environments. The core of Ethereum is not fundamentally different from the Bitcoin system itself. But it supports contract formation which makes blockchains not only digital encryption currencies but also offers more commercial non-commercial application scenarios.

2.4.4 Blockchain 3.0

After the gradual maturation of Bitcoin, the concept of cryptocurrency has gradually gained recognition and acceptance. Within a few years since 2011, digital currencies such as Litecoin, Ripple, R3, and blockchain technologies have emerged in competition. At the same time, Germany officially recognised Bitcoin, and Nasdaq completed the transaction through its own blockchain platform. Although the people's Bank of China denied the status of Bitcoin, it was the only bank in the world that immediately announced that it would become its own cryptocurrency/digital currency. According to statistics, as of April this year, 455 blockchain companies in the world have obtained nearly $2 billion of investment, of which 61 can be counted in China. On the whole, driven by some giants such as Bitcoin and Ethereum, a wave of digital currency and blockchain has begun in the world.

It is no longer enough to describe the general picture of this new era through a simple timeline. Therefore, I divide the analysis of blockchain into four dimensions: technology, industry, government, and society.

From the perspective of technology, in the era of blockchain, Ethereum, Corda, and ZCash are emerging together. The consensus mechanism of blockchain technology is also becoming mature, and there are many sects and categories. At the same time, Bitcoin's global computing power has reached 4 EH/s, which shows that digital currency and blockchain technology have entered an era of rapid growth.

From the perspective of the industry, blockchain has successful POC cases in more than a dozen fields around the world, such as bills, securities, insurance, supply chain, deposit certificate, traceability, and intellectual property rights, and some of them have entered the practical stage. Not only independent developers but also a number of domestic and international large financial institutions, banks and traditional enterprises have also established their own blockchain projects. Whether it is their own R&D or cooperation with a third party, it proves that the application of blockchain technology in the industry is also a hot trend.

From the government's point of view, as far as Bitcoin is concerned, more than a dozen countries in the world recognise that it has the status of currency or similar currency and can be traded and circulated. China's central bank, although it forbids the circulation of Bitcoin, is very radical in declaring that it wants to be a digital currency.

Google Scholar has almost reached 20,000 academic papers related to blockchain, we can see that blockchain technology is no longer a technology attached to Bitcoin, Ethereum, or any digital currency but is really brought into the academic research field as an independent technology.

2.5 CHAPTER SUMMARY

The blockchain idea is born out of the quest for more advanced distributed bookkeeping technology. Bitcoin network is the first distributed ledger system with self-trust and tamper-proof. This makes people realise that in addition to the best-effort (not guaranteed trusted) infrastructure such as the Internet, the blockchain technology will also have the potential to shape a future network infrastructure that trusts each other.

Digital currencies are the driving force behind the birth of the blockchain, and it is the constant search for solutions to implement digital currencies that eventually led to the creation of Bitcoin and also marked the birth of the blockchain. In the field of digital currencies, although only digital cryptocurrencies with blockchain technology at their core have achieved the ultimate victory, other disappearing digital currencies have left behind a number of very practical technologies.

In addition to digital currency applications, the industry is increasingly looking at the potential of blockchain technology in business scenarios. Open-source community-initiated projects such as Ethereum and hyperledger provide solid platform support for more complex distributed ledger applications.

Distributed systems are a very important area of computer science. As the size of clusters continues to grow, the amount of data processed is increasing, and the requirements for performance and reliability are increasing, the technologies related to distributed systems have become increasingly important and play a significantly critical role.

The classical problem of how to ensure consensus in distributed systems is of high research value, both academically and in engineering terms. Unfortunately, the ideal (optimal in all metrics) solution does not exist. Under a variety of realistic constraints, it is often necessary to design protocols that satisfy specific scenarios by sacrificing certain requirements. In this chapter, the reader will be able to appreciate similar design techniques in engineering applications.

In fact, many problems in engineering do not have a one-size-fits-all universal solution; the practical solution ideas are all about making a reasonably flexible trade-off between practical requirements and constraints.

The existing results of modern cryptography have been heavily utilised in blockchain, in turn, the application of blockchain in many scenarios has created many new demands and contributed to the further development of the security discipline.

Bitcoin itself, as a major breakthrough in the field of digital currency, has a profound impact on the field of distributed bookkeeping. In particular, its underlying blockchain technology has been valued by the financial and information industries and has been applied in many scenarios.

The Ethereum project extends the blockchain technology on the basis of digital currency, proposes the grand idea of creating a more universal smart contract platform, and builds an open-source ecosystem based on the open-source technology with Ethereum at its core.

REFERENCES

Beck, R., Czepluch, J. S., Lollike, N., & Malone, S. (2016). Blockchain - The gateway to trust-free cryptographic transactions. *Twenty-fourth European Conference on Information Systems*, 18(4), 315–319.

Birgit, C., & Ruth, B. (2018). Blockchain, IP and the pharma industry—how distributed ledger technologies can help secure the pharma supply chain. *Journal of Intellectual Property Law & Practice*, 13(7), 531-533.

Chandan, A., Potdar, V., & Rosano, M. (2020). How blockchain can help in supply chain sustainability. *Australasian Conference on Information Systems 2019*, 12(5), 51–58.

Conti, M., Kumar, E. S., Lal, C., & Ruj, S. (2018). A survey on security and privacy issues of bitcoin. *IEEE Communications Surveys & Tutorial*, 7(4), 15–19.

Dinh, T. T. A., Wang, J., Chen, G., Liu, R., & Tan, K. L. (2017). BLOCKBENCH: A framework for analyzing private blockchains. *The 2017 ACM International Conference*, 5(12), 205–209.

Dutta, P., Choi, T. M., Somani, S., & Butala, R. (2020). Blockchain technology in supply chain operations: Applications, challenges and research opportunities. *Transportation Research Part E Logs and Transportation Review*, 6(15), 33–38.

Gervais, A., Karame, G. O., Wüst, K., Glykantzis, V., & Capkun, S. (2016). On the Security and Performance of Proof of Work Blockchains. *ACM Sigsac Conference on Computer & Communications Security*, 8(15), 86–96.

Kocher, P. C. (1996). Timing attacks on implementations of diffie-hellman, rsa, dss, and other systems. *CRYPTO*, 23(12), 367–369.

Kosba, A., Miller, A., Shi, E., Wen, Z., & Papamanthou, C. (2016). Hawk: The blockchain model of cryptography and privacy-preserving smart contracts. *Security & Privacy*, 17(17), 161–166.

Lamport, L., Shostak, R., & Pease, M. (2019). The Byzantine generals problem. *In Concurrency: the Works of Leslie Lamport* (pp. 203–226).

Lemieux, V. L. (2016). Trusting records: Is blockchain technology the answer? *Records Management Journal*, 26(2), 110-139.

Mijovic, M., Miletic, A., Dimitrijevic, B., Stojanovic, J. R., Zivanovic, M., & Cuturilo, G. (2019). Three patients with pyridoxine-dependent epilepsy—Psychological, ethical and professional issues in diagnostic approach as a proof of importance of pre and post-test genetic counseling. *European Journal of Human Genetics*, 27, 734-735.

Pass, R., Seeman, L., & Shelat, A. (2017). Analysis of the blockchain protocol in asynchronous networks. *Annual International Conference on the Theory and Applications of Cryptographic Techniques*, 2(5), 310–319.

Paul, G., Sarkar, P., & Mukherjee, S. (2014). Towards a more democratic mining in bitcoins. *International Conference on Information Systems Security*, 14(7), 120–123.

Peters, G., & Panayi, E. (2015). Understanding modern banking ledgers through blockchain technologies: Future of transaction processing and smart contracts on the internet of money. *Social Science Electronic Publishing, 7*(15), 211–217.

Radziwill, N. (2018). Blockchain revolution: how the technology behind bitcoin is changing money, business, and the world. *Quality Management Journal, 25*(1), 64-65.

Saleh, F. (2018). *Blockchain without waste: proof-of-stake.* Social Science Electronic Publishing.

Wang, T., Bai, X., Wang, H., Liew, S. C., & Zhang, S. (2020). Game-theoretical analysis of mining strategy for bitcoin-ng blockchain protocol. *IEEE Systems Journal*, PP(99), 1-12.

Watanabe, H., Fujimura, S., Nakadaira, A., Miyazaki, Y., Akutsu, A., & Kishigami, J. (2016). Blockchain contract: Securing a blockchain applied to smart contracts. *IEEE International Conference on Consumer Electronics* (pp. 467-468). IEEE.

Evolution of Two Technologies

3.1 DEVELOPMENT TREND OF BIG DATA TECHNOLOGY

In the era of big data, traditional software has been unable to process and mine information in large amounts of data. The most important change is Google's 'three carriages'. Google has successively released Google's distributed file system (GFS), big data distributed computing framework MapReduce, and big data NoSQL database BigTable around 2004. These three papers have laid the cornerstone of big data technology. As we know, search engines mainly do two things, one is web page fetching, and the other is index building. In this process, there is a large amount of data to be stored and calculated. These three technologies are actually designed to solve this problem. We can also tell by the name, a file system, a computing framework, and a database system. Changes are always dominated by big companies like Google. At that time, when most companies were still working on improving single-machine performance, Google had begun to envision the distribution of data storage and calculations to a large number of cheap computers to execute. Because of that time period, most companies actually focused on a single machine, thinking about how to improve the performance of a single machine and looking for more expensive and better servers. Google's idea is to deploy a large-scale server cluster, store massive amounts of data on this cluster in a distributed manner, and then use all machines on the cluster for data calculations. In this way, Google doesn't actually need to buy a lot of expensive servers. It only needs to organise these ordinary machines together, which is very powerful.

Inspired by Google's paper, in July 2004, Doug Cutting and Mike Cafarella implemented GFS-like functions in Nutch, the predecessor of later Hadoop Distributed File System (HDFS). Later in February 2005, Mike Cafarella implemented the original version of MapReduce in Nutch. By 2006, Hadoop was separated from Nutch and started an independent project. The open-source of Hadoop promoted the vigorous development of the big data industry and brought a profound technological revolution. If you have time, you can simply browse the Hadoop code, the pure software written in Java has no advanced technical difficulties and use also some of the most basic programming skills; there is nothing surprising, but it can bring huge influence to the society, even to drive a profound revolution of science and technology, and promote the development and progress of artificial intelligence.

Next, big data-related technologies continue to develop, and the open-source approach has gradually formed a big data ecosystem. Because MapReduce programming is cumbersome, Facebook contributes Hive, and SQL syntax provides great help for data analysis and data mining. Cloudera, the first commercial company to operate Hadoop, was also established in 2008.

Since memory hardware had broken through cost constraints, Spark gradually replaced MapReduce's status in 2014 and was sought after by the industry. The operation speed of Spark running programs in memory can be 100 times faster than that of Hadoop MapReduce, and its operation mode is suitable for machine learning tasks. Spark was born in UC Berkeley AMPLab in 2009, open-sourced in 2010, and contributed to the Apache Foundation in 2013.

Both Spark and MapReduce are focused on offline calculations, usually, tens of minutes or longer, and are batch programs. Due to the demand for real-time computing, streaming computing engines have begun to appear, including Storm, Flink, and Spark Streaming.

The development of big data storage and processing technology has also spurred the vigorous development of data analysis and machine learning and has also prompted the emergence of emerging industries. Big data technology is the cornerstone, and the landing of artificial intelligence is the next outlet. Being in the Internet industry and feeling that the technology is progressing quickly, we should ignore the impetuousness and grasp the change.

Big data needs to cope with quantified and fast-growing storage, which requires the underlying hardware architecture and file system to be significantly higher than traditional technologies in terms of cost performance and able to elastically expand storage capacity. One challenge that big data poses to storage technology is the ability to adapt to multiple data formats. Therefore, the storage layer of big data is not only HDFS of Hadoop but also storage architectures such as HBase and Kudu.

3.2 KEY TECHNOLOGIES OF BIG DATA

From the perspective of the life cycle of data, big data needs to go through several links from the analysis and mining of data sources to finally generate value, including data generation, data storage, data analysis, and data utilisation, as shown in Figure 3.1.

Big data needs to cope with quantified and fast-growing storage, which requires the underlying hardware architecture and file system to be much higher in cost performance than traditional technologies and able to elastically expand storage capacity. Google's GFS and Hadoop's HDFS laid the foundation for big data storage technology. In addition, another challenge that big data poses to storage technologies is the ability to adapt to

FIGURE 3.1   Big data lifecycle.

multiple data formats. Therefore, the underlying storage layer of big data is not only HDFS but also storage architectures such as HBase and Kudu.

Blockchain is essentially a distributed database system. As a kind of chained access data technology, blockchain technology participates in the calculation and recording of data through multiple nodes participating in the calculation in the network and verifies the validity of its information with each other. From this point, the blockchain technology is also a specific database technology. Due to the characteristics of decentralised databases in terms of security and convenience, many people in the industry are optimistic about the development of blockchain and believe that blockchain is an upgrade and supplement to the existing Internet technology.

3.2.1 Hadoop

Hadoop is an open-source distributed computing platform provided by the Apache Software Foundation. It can provide users with a distributed infrastructure with transparent system details and make full use of the cluster method for storage and high-speed calculations.

Applications working in the Hadoop framework can work in an environment that provides distributed storage and computing across computer clusters. Hadoop is designed to scale from a single server to thousands of machines, and each machine provides local computing and storage.

The Hadoop framework includes the following four modules:

Hadoop Common: These are the Java libraries and utilities required by other Hadoop modules. These libraries provide the file system and operating system-level abstractions and contain the necessary Java files and scripts needed to start Hadoop.

Hadoop YARN: This is a framework for job scheduling and cluster resource management.

HDFS: A distributed file system that provides high-throughput access to application data.

Hadoop MapReduce: This is a parallel processing system for large data sets based on YARN.

We can use the following diagram to describe the four components available in the Hadoop framework, as shown in Figure 3.2.

Hadoop implements the distributed file system HDFS. HBase is a NoSQL database based on HDFS that has been listed as the centre. It is used to quickly read and write large amounts of data and is managed by

FIGURE 3.2   Hadoop architecture.

Zookeeper. HDFS not only simplifies the requirements of POSIX but also allows streaming access to the related data in the file system.

The original goal of Hadoop design is high reliability, high scalability, high fault tolerance, and high efficiency. The unique advantage of the design is that with the emergence of Hadoop, many large companies will fall into trouble. At the same time, it has also aroused widespread interest in the research community. Due to the unique advantages of data extraction, conversion, and loading, Hadoop can be widely used in big data processing applications. The distributed architecture of Hadoop makes the big data processing engine as close to the storage as possible. The batch results of these processes can be moved directly to storage, making them relatively suitable for batch processing tasks.

The advantages of the Hadoop platform:

1. High scalability: Theoretically, it can be unlimited. Because in the Hadoop test framework, performance and capacity can be improved by simply adding some hardware.

2. Low cost: You don't need to rely on high-end hardware. As long as ordinary PCs, the entire system is stacked by cheap machines, and the reliability of the system is ensured through software fault tolerance.

3. Mature ecosystem: Open-source, with many tools (HIVE), which lowers the threshold for using Hadoop and improves the applicability of Hadoop.

3.2.2 MapReduce

Hadoop MapReduce is a software framework for easily writing applications. It processes large amounts of data on large clusters (thousands of nodes) in a reliable and fault-tolerant manner and processes commodity hardware in parallel.

The term MapReduce actually refers to the following two different tasks performed by the Hadoop program:

Map Task: This is the first task, which receives input data and converts it into a set of data, where individual elements are decomposed into tuples (key/value).

Reduce Task: This task takes the output of the map task as input and combines these data elements into a smaller set of tuples. The reduce task is always executed after the map task.

Usually, the input and output are stored in the file system. The framework is responsible for scheduling tasks, monitoring them and re-executing failed tasks.

The MapReduce framework consists of a single master JobTracker and a slave TaskTracker for each cluster node. The supervisor is responsible for resource management, tracking resource consumption/availability, scheduling job component tasks on the slave station, and monitoring and re-executing fault tasks. The slave TaskTracker performs tasks according to the instructions of the host and periodically provides task status information to the master device. JobTracker is a single point of failure for the Hadoop MapReduce service, which means that if JobTracker is shut down, all running jobs will stop.

Hadoop's MapReduce function recognises the interruption of a single job, sends the scattered jobs to multiple nodes, and then reduces them to the data warehouse in the form of a single data set. By using the MapReduce framework, people can easily develop distributed systems and only write their own Map and Reduce functions to perform big data measurement and processing. In order for the client to write files into HDFS, they must be cached in local temporary storage. If the cached data is larger than the required HDFS block size, the file creation request will be sent to the NameNode. The NameNode responds to the client with the DataNode ID and target block. When the client starts sending temporary files to the first DataNode, it will immediately pipe the contents of the block to the DataNode replica.

All of the above are theoretical explanations of MapReduce, so let's understand the problem in terms of the process and code generated by MapReduce. If you want to count the most words that have appeared in computer papers over the past 10 years and see what everyone has been working on, what should you do once you have collected your papers?

Method 1: You can write a small program that goes through all the papers in order, counts the number of occurrences of each encountered word, and finally you will know which words are the most popular. This method is very effective and the simplest to implement when the data set is small, and is appropriate for solving this problem.

Method 2: Write a multi-threaded program that traverses the papers concurrently. This problem can theoretically be highly concurrent since counting one file does not affect counting another file. When our machine is multi-core or multi-processor, method two are definitely more efficient than method one. But writing a multi-threaded program is much more difficult than method one, we have to synchronise and share the data ourselves, for example, to prevent two threads from double counting the file.

Method 3: Give the assignment to multiple computers to complete. We can use the program from method one, deploy it to N machines, and then split the proceedings into N copies, with one machine running one job. This method runs fast enough, but it's a pain to deploy, we have to manually copy the program to another machine, we have to manually separate the proceedings, and most painful of all, we have to integrate the results of the N runs (we can write another program, of course).

Method 4: Let MapReduce help us out. MapReduce is essentially method three, but how to split a fileset, how to copy the program, how to integrate the results are all defined by the framework. We just define this task (the user program) and leave the rest to MapReduce.

The map function: accepts a key-value pair (key-value pair), resulting in a set of intermediate key-value pairs. The MapReduce framework will map function generated by the intermediate key-value pairs of the same key value is passed to a reduce function.

The reduce function: accepts a key, and a set of related values (value list), the set of values will be merged to produce a smaller set of values (usually only one or zero values).

The core code of the statistical word frequency MapReduce function is very short, mainly to implement these two functions.

```
map(String key, String value):
        // key: document name
        // value: document contents
        for each word w in value:
            EmitIntermediate(w, "1");
```

```
reduce(String key, Iterator values):
    // key: a word
    // values: a list of counts
    int result = 0;
    for each v in values:
            result += ParseInt(v);
    Emit(AsString(result));
```

In the example of the word count, the map function accepts the key as the file name and the value as the file's contents. Map traverses the words one by one, generating an intermediate key-value pair <w, '1'> for each word it encounters (indicating that we have found another word w); MapReduce passes the same key-value pair (both words w) to reduce. function, so that the reduce function accepts the key as the word w, the value is a series of '1' (the most basic implementation is like this, but can be optimised), the number of keys equal to the number of key-value pairs with the key w, and then accumulate these '1' to get the number of occurrences of the word w. Finally, the number of occurrences of the word w is written to the underlying distributed storage system (GFS or HDFS), and is stored in the user-defined location. These occurrences are written to a user-defined location and stored in the underlying distributed storage system (GFS or HDFS).

3.2.3 Spark

Spark, as Apache's top open-source project, is a fast and versatile large-scale data processing engine. It is similar to Hadoop's MapReduce computing framework. However, compared to MapReduce, Spark has its scalability, in-memory computing, and other features. The advantages of data in any format on Hadoop are more efficient when batch processing, and have lower latency. Relative to the goal of 'one stack to rule all', in fact, Spark has become a unified platform for rapid processing of lightweight big data. Various applications, such as real-time stream processing, machine learning, interactive query, etc. It can be built on different storage and running systems through Spark.

Spark is a big data-parallel computing framework based on in-memory computing. Spark is based on in-memory computing, which improves the real-time performance of data processing in a big data environment, and at the same time guarantees high fault tolerance and high scalability, allowing users to deploy Spark on a large number of cheap hardware to form a cluster.

Compared to most big data processing frameworks, Spark is becoming one of the new and most influential big data frameworks after Hadoop's MapReduce with its excellent low-latency performance. The entire eco-system with Spark as the core, the bottom layer is the distributed storage system HDFS, Amazon S3, Mesos, or other format storage systems (such as HBase); resource management adopts cluster resource management models such as Mesos, YARN, or Spark comes with independent operating mode, as well as local operating mode. In the Spark big data processing framework, Spark provides services for a variety of upper-layer applications. For example, Spark SQL provides SQL query services, performance is 3– 50 times faster than Hive; MLlib provides machine learning services; GraphX provides graph computing services; Spark Streaming decomposes streaming computing into a series of short batch calculations, and provides high reliability and throughput service. It is worth noting that whether it is Spark SQL, Spark Streaming, GraphX or MLlib, you can use the Spark core API to deal with problems. Their methods are almost universal, and the processed data can also be shared, which not only reduces the learning cost but also its data Seamless integration greatly improves flexibility.

Spark has the following key features.

Running fast: Spark uses an advanced DAG (Directed Acyclic Graph) execution engine to support cyclic data flows and in-memory computations, with memory-based execution up to a hundred times faster than Hadoop MapReduce and up to ten times faster than disk-based execution.

Ease of use: Spark supports programming in Scala, Java, Python, and R. The simple API design helps users easily build parallel programs and allows for interactive programming through the Spark Shell.

Versatility: Spark provides a complete and powerful technology stack, including SQL queries, streaming computing, machine learning, and graph algorithm components that can be seamlessly integrated into the same application and are robust enough to handle complex computations.

Various operating modes: Spark can run in a standalone clustered mode, or in Hadoop, or in cloud environments such as Amazon EC2, and can access a variety of data sources such as HDFS, Cassandra, HBase, Hive, and more.

Figure 3.3 shows the architectural design of The Spark. The Spark runtime architecture includes a Cluster Manager, a Worker Node to run job tasks, a Driver for each application, and an Executor for specific tasks on

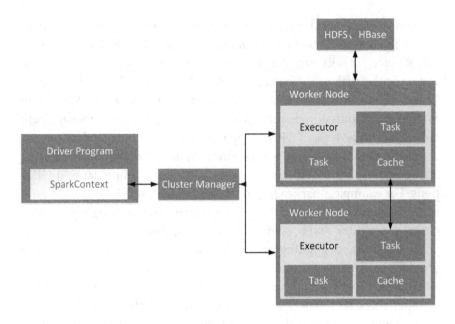

FIGURE 3.3   Spark architecture design.

each Worker Node. The Cluster Manager can be Spark's own resource manager or a resource management framework such as YARN or Mesos.

3.3 DEVELOPMENT OF BLOCKCHAIN TECHNOLOGY

Blockchain is essentially a distributed database system. As a kind of chain access data technology, blockchain technology participates in the calculation and recording of data through multiple nodes participating in the calculation in the network and verifies the validity of its information with each other. From this point of view, blockchain technology is also a specific database technology, which has played a great role in upgrading and supplementing existing Internet technologies.

In 1976, two masters of cryptography, Bailey W. Diffie and Martin E. Hellman published a paper 'New Directions in Cryptography', which covered all the new development areas of cryptography in the coming decades, including asymmetric encryption, Elliptic curve algorithms, hashing and other means have laid the development direction of the entire cryptography so far, and also played a decisive role in the development of blockchain technology and the birth of Bitcoin.

Immediately after in 1977, the famous RSA algorithm was born. It was not surprising that the three inventors won the Turing Award in 2002. However, the patents they applied for RSA, in the world generally recognised that the algorithm cannot apply for patents, really no one admits, and it expired in 2000 in advance. In 1980, Merkle Ralf proposed the Merkle-Tree data structure and the corresponding algorithm. One of the main uses later was to verify the correctness of data synchronisation in distributed networks. It was worth noting that in 1980, the really popular hash algorithm and distributed network have not yet appeared, for example: the well-known SHA-1, MD5 and other things were born in the 1990s. In that era, Merkle released such a data structure, which later played an important role in the field of cryptography and distributed computing, which is somewhat surprising. However, if you understand the background of Merkle, you know that this is no accident: He is a doctoral student of Hellman, one of the two authors of 'New Directions in Cryptography' (the other author, Diffie is a research assistant of Hellman). 'New Directions in Cryptography' is the research direction of Merkle Ralf's doctoral students. It is said that Merkle is actually one of the main authors of 'New Directions in Cryptography'. It was only because he was a doctoral student at the time that he did not receive the invitation to the academic conference to publish this paper. Turing Award missed.

In 1982, Lamport raised the question of General Byzantium, marking that the reliability theory and practice of distributed computing have entered a substantial stage. In the same year, David Chom proposed the cryptographic payment system ECash. It can be seen that with the progress of cryptography, keen people have begun to try to apply it to the fields of currency and payment. It should be said that ECash is a cryptography One of the earliest pioneers in encryption currency.

In 1985, Koblitz and Miller independently proposed the famous elliptic curve encryption (ECC) algorithm. Because the RSA algorithm previously invented is too large to calculate, it is difficult to be practical. The proposal of ECC really makes the asymmetric encryption system practical. Therefore, it could be said that in 1985, about 10 years after the publication of 'New Directions in Cryptography', the theoretical and technical foundation of modern cryptography had been fully established.

Interestingly, during the period from 1985 to 1997, there were no particularly significant developments in cryptography, distributed networks, and relations with payment/currency. In the author's opinion, this phenomenon is easy to understand: when new ideas, concepts, and technologies are created, there must always be a considerable amount of time for everyone to learn, explore, and practice, and then there may be breakthrough results. The first 10 years are often the development of theory, and the latter 10 years have entered the stage of practical exploration. The period of about 1985–1997 should be the stage of the rapid development of related fields in practice. Finally, starting from 1976, after about 20 years, the field of cryptography and distributed computing finally entered an explosive period.

In 1997, the HashCash method, which was the first generation of POW (Proof of Work) algorithm, appeared at that time and was mainly used for anti-spam. In various papers published later, the specific algorithm design and implementation have completely covered the POW mechanism used by Bitcoin later.

By 1998, the complete idea of cryptocurrency finally came out, and Wei Dai and Nick Sabo simultaneously proposed the concept of cryptocurrency. Among them, Dai Wei's B-Money was called the spiritual pioneer of Bitcoin, and Nick Sabo's Bitgold outline was very close to the characteristics listed in Satoshi's Bitcoin paper, so that some people once suspected that Sabo was Satoshi. Interestingly, it was another 10 years since the birth of Bitcoin.

With the advent of the 21st century, there have been several major developments in the blockchain-related field: First, the peer-to-peer distributed network. During the three years from 1999 to 2001, Napster, Edonkey 2000, and BitTorrent emerged one after another. The basis of P2P network computing.

Another important thing in 2001 was that the NSA released the SHA-2 series of algorithms, including the currently most widely used SHA-256 algorithm, which was the hash algorithm finally adopted by Bitcoin. It should be said that in 2001, all the technical foundations of the birth of Bitcoin or blockchain technology were solved in theory and practice, and Bitcoin was ready to come out. This phenomenon was often seen in human history. It takes about 30 years from the time when an idea or technology is proposed to its true development.

This phenomenon is not uncommon not only in the field of technology but also in other fields such as philosophy, natural sciences, and mathematics. The emergence and development of blockchain also follow this model. This model is also easy to understand, because after the birth of an idea, an algorithm, and a technology, it must be digested, explored, and practiced, and it takes roughly a generation of time.

Satoshi Nakamoto published the famous paper 'Bitcoin: A Peer-to-Peer Electronic Cash System' in November 2008. In January 2009, the founding block was excavated with his first version of the software, containing this sentence: 'The Times 03/Jan/2009 Chancellor on brink of second bailout for banks'. Opened the era of Bitcoin like a curse. For the development process of Bitcoin, there are several time nodes that I think are important.

In September 2010, the first mining site Slush invented the method of multiple nodes cooperative mining, which became the beginning of the industry of Bitcoin mining. You should know that before May 2010, 10,000 bitcoins were only worth $25. If calculated at this price, all bitcoins (21 million) would also be worth $50,000. Concentrating on mining is obviously meaningless. Therefore, the decision to establish a mining pool means that someone believes that Bitcoin will become a virtual currency that can be exchanged with real-world currencies and has unlimited growth space in the future. This is undoubtedly a vision.

In April 2011, the first version officially recorded by Bitcoin official: 0.3.21 was released. This version was very junior, but of great significance. First of all, because he supports uPNP and realises the ability of the P2P software we use every day, Bitcoin could really enter the room and enter the home of ordinary people so that anyone could participate in the transaction. Secondly, before this, the smallest unit of bitcoin node only supported 0.01 bitcoin, which was equivalent to 'point', and this version really supports 'satoshi'. It could be said that since this version, Bitcoin had become what it was now, and it had really formed the market. Before this, it was basically a plaything for technicians.

In 2013, Bitcoin released version 0.8, which was the most important version in the history of Bitcoin. It had completely improved the internal management of the Bitcoin node itself and the optimisation of network communication. It was after this point in time that Bitcoin really supported large-scale transactions across the entire network, becoming the electronic cash envisioned by Satoshi Nakamoto, and truly having global influence.

Things have not always been smooth. In the most important version 0.8, Bitcoin encountered a big bug, so after this version is released, Bitcoin had a hard fork in a short time, resulting in the entire Bitcoin finally having to fall back to the old version, this also led to a sharp drop in the price of Bitcoin.

The development after Bitcoin is well known by more and more people. For example, the attitudes of countries around the world, the growth of computing power-reached 1EH/S in January 2016, and more than 10,000 related open-source projects prove that the Bitcoin ecosystem was fully mature.

Everyone is familiar with Ethereum, and the second-largest digital currency in circulation is second only to Bitcoin. Known as Blockchain 2.0. Ethereum was invented by Vitalik Buterin. This Russian guy did development and news reports in the field of Bitcoin very early and finally developed Ethereum on his own. At the end of 2013, Vitalik Buterin described Ethereum for the first time as a result of his research on the Bitcoin community. Soon after, Vitalik published an Ethereum white paper 'The structure of smart contracts'. In January 2014, Vitalik officially announced Ethereum at the North American Bitcoin Conference in Miami, Florida.

Ethereum is divided into four stages, Frontier, Homestead, Metropolis, Serenity, the transition between stages needs to be achieved through a hard fork. The first three phases use a proof of work (POW) system, and the last phase uses a proof of stake (POS) system.

At the same time, Vitalik started working with Dr. Gavin Wood to create Ethereum. In April 2014, Gavin published the Ethereum Yellow Book as a technical description of the Ethereum virtual machine. According to the specific instructions in the Yellow Book, the Ethereum client has been implemented in seven programming languages (C++, Go, Python, Java, JavaScript, Haskell, Rust), making the software more optimised overall. It improves the compatibility of Ethereum development and provides a solid foundation for the later development of Ethereum. Multiple development teams located in many countries can implement the same Ethereum protocol in different programming languages, so that Ethereum can be integrated into other systems as widely as possible, providing long-term flexibility and being suitable for the future.

The consortium blockchain is called Blockchain 3.0. Blockchain is towards more complex intelligent contracts, hyperledger in the future can record anything that can be expressed in the form of code, expand the application to the government, health, science, art, etc.

It can be said that blockchain has already built a potential value interconnection layer beyond information interconnection based on the bottom layer of the Internet. Hyperledger, led by IBM, is arguably the current leader.

In December 2015, led by the Linux Foundation, IBM, Intel, Cisco, and others jointly announced the establishment of the Hyperledger joint project. The hyperledger project provides an open-source reference implementation for transparent, open, decentralised enterprise distributed ledger technology. The hyperledger introduced the blockchain technology into the application scenario of distributed alliance ledger for the first time, laying a foundation for building a highly efficient commercial network based on the blockchain technology in the future. Currently, the hyperledger consists of eight top sub-projects for different purposes and scenarios:

- Fabric: the target is the basic core platform of blockchain, which supports permission management and is realised based on Go language;

- Sawtooth: support the brand new hardware chip-based consensus mechanism, Proof of Elapsed Time (PoET);

- Iroha: ledger platform project, based on C++ implementation, with Web and mobile-oriented features;

- Blockchain Explorer: provides a Web interface to view the status (block number, transaction history) information of the query binding Blockchain;

- Cello: provide the deployment and runtime management functions of the blockchain platform. Application developers need not care how to build and maintain the blockchain

- Indy: provides a digital identity management mechanism based on distributed ledger technology;

- Composer: provides high-level language support for the development of chaincode, automatically generates chaincode, etc.;

- Burrow: provides support for Ethereum virtual machines to implement a privileged blockchain platform for efficient trading.

The logical architecture of Fabric is the technical component. From the application, including the SDK, API, events, and through the SDK, API, events on the underlying blockchain operation: including identity management, ledger management, contract management, intelligent deployment, and call. From the point of the underlying blockchain, this end

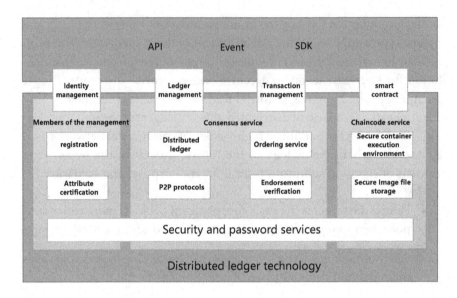

FIGURE 3.4 The basic framework of fabric.

provides the following services: member management service, consensus, chaincode, security, and password services. Fabric provides pluggability and flexibility by separating parts into modules. The basic framework of Fabric is as showed in Figure 3.4.

3.4 TAXONOMY OF BLOCKCHAIN SYSTEMS

Current blockchain systems can be roughly categorised into three types: public blockchain, private blockchain and consortium blockchain (Buterin, 2014). We compare these three types of blockchain from different perspectives (Zheng, Xie, Dai, Chen, & Wang, 2018). The comparison is listed in Table 3.1.

Consensus determination. In public blockchain, each node could take part in the consensus process. And only a selected set of nodes are responsible for validating the block in consortium blockchain. As for private chain, it is fully controlled by one organisation who could determine the final consensus.

Read permission. Transactions in a public blockchain are visible to the public while the read permission depends on a private blockchain or a consortium blockchain. The consortium or the organisation could decide whether the stored information is public or restricted.

TABLE 3.1 Comparisons Among Public Blockchain, Consortium Blockchain and Private Blockchain

Property	Public Blockchain	Consortium Blockchain	Private Blockchain
Consensus determination	All miners	Selected set of nodes	One organisation
Read permission	Public	Could be public or restricted	Could be public or restricted
Immutability	Nearly impossible to tamper	Could be tampered	Tampered
Efficiency	Low	High	High
Centralised	No	Partial	Yes
Consensus process	Permissionless	Permissioned	Permissioned

Immutability. Since transactions are stored in different nodes in the distributed network, so it is nearly impossible to tamper the public blockchain. However, if the majority of the consortium or the dominant organisation wants to tamper the blockchain, the consortium blockchain or private blockchain could be reversed or tampered.

Efficiency. It takes plenty of time to propagate transactions and blocks as there are a large number of nodes on public blockchain network. Taking network safety into consideration, restrictions on public blockchain would be much more strict. As a result, transaction throughput is limited and the latency is high. With fewer validators, consortium blockchain and private blockchain could be more efficient.

Centralised. The main difference among the three types of blockchains is that public blockchain is decentralised, consortium blockchain is partially centralised and private blockchain is fully centralised as it is controlled by a single group.

Consensus process. Everyone in the world could join the consensus process of the public blockchain. Different from public blockchain, both consortium blockchain and private blockchain are permissioned. One node needs to be certificated to join the consensus process in consortium or private blockchain.

Since public blockchain is open to the world, it can attract many users. Communities are also very active. Many public blockchains emerge day by day. As for consortium blockchain, it could be applied to many business applications. Currently, Hyperledger (Androulaki et al., 2018) is developing business consortium blockchain frameworks. Ethereum also has provided tools for building consortium blockchains. As for private blockchain, there are still many companies implementing it for efficiency and auditability.

3.5 SCALABILITY OF BLOCKCHAIN TECHNOLOGY

Currently, the blockchain scalability bottleneck is mainly in three aspects: performance inefficiency, high confirmation delay, and function extension. For example, Bitcoin can only deal with seven transactions per second on average. Obviously, it cannot meet the requirement of current digital payment scenarios, nor can it be carried in other applications such as distributed storage and credit service. Here are four mainstream solutions to improve the performance of blockchain system, including the sharding mechanism, DAG-based, off-chain payment network, and cross-chain technology.

3.5.1 Sharding Mechanism

In 2016, Luu et al. published a paper, which proposed the concept of Sharding in the field of blockchain for the first time. Its general design idea is: Turn each block in the blockchain network into a sub-blockchain, and sub-blockchain can accommodate several (currently 100) collation packaged with transaction data. These collations finally constitute a block on the main chain; because this collation exists as a whole in a block, its data must be packaged and generated by a specific miner, essentially the same as the blocks in the existing protocol, so no additional network confirmation is required. That would increase the trading capacity of each block by about 100 times.

Elastico and Zilliqa are two typical projects using the sharding mechanism. They both adopt PoW to prove as Sharding algorithm, and the scheme during the consensus adopted PBFT algorithm. In order to resist the Sybil attack, at the beginning of a consensus, nodes need to conduct simple work to prove to get involved in PBFT identity. The criteria for dividing nodes into different sets are based on the result of PoW. By establishing a probability model, it can be obtained that when the sharding size reaches 600, the probability that the attacker can control a sharding (i.e. having more than 1/3 nodes in any shard) is negligible, even if the attacker has 1/3 computing power. The specific process can be abstracted as follows:

1. The node obtains its identity through PoW and divides it into different sets.

2. Conduct transaction consensus within each sharding through PBFT algorithm.

3. The transaction set after the consensus segmentation and the signature in the consensus process are broadcast to a certain shard. The shard verifies the signature, conducts the consensus segmentation, and packages the consensus into blocks and broadcasts the whole network.

Elastico's solution is based on the UTXO model. By making transactions on the main chain and creating a receipt (with receiptID), the user can store the data in a specified sharding. And the user on the Sharding chain can create a receipt-consuming transaction to spend the receipt given receiptID. Elastico can therefore effectively resist double-spend attack during transaction processing so that when processing a trade, it maps to different Sharding processes via the input to the trade as a baseline.

Zilliqa is a solution model based on the account model. When the transaction processing, it maps to different shards by the identity of the sender. In the consensus process, different sender trading could be mapped to different subdivisions (different validations), but the same sender transactions will be handled by the same sharding, so the trusted nodes in the sharding are determined to the state of a particular sender. Therefore, it can resist a double-spend attack model based on the account.

3.5.2 DAG-based

Using a DAG as a distributed ledger is not about removing proof-of-work mining, blocks, or transaction fees. It is about leveraging the structural properties of DAGs to potentially solve blockchain's orphan rate problem. The ability of a DAG to withstand this problem and thus improve on scalability is contingent on the additional rules implemented to deal with transaction consistency, and any other design choices made.

The DAG blockchain mainly improves the data layer and consensus layer of bitcoin blockchain, as shown in Figure 3.5. It follows the P2P network structure of bitcoin blockchain to organise the nodes of the whole network. On the bitcoin blockchain, newly released blocks will be added to the original longest chain, which will be extended indefinitely according to the longest chain considered by all nodes.

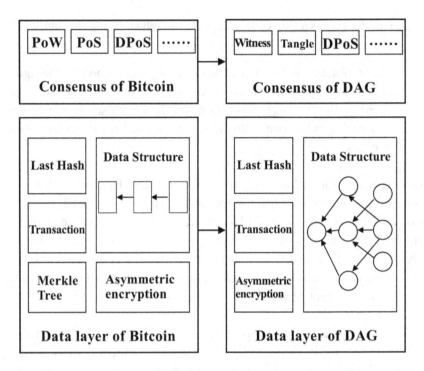

FIGURE 3.5 The difference between DAG and Bitcoin.

3.5.3 Off-Chain Payment Network

Such solutions are generally proposed on the original public chain, such as Bitcoin's Lightning Network and Ethereum's Raiden Network, which mainly solve the payment problem.

The two strategies are to keep the underlying blockchain protocol unchanged, put transactions under the chain for execution, and solve scalability problems by changing the way the protocol is used. The part of the off-chain can be implemented with the traditional centralised distributed system, and the performance is scalable. Under this strategy, only coarse-grained ledgers are recorded on the distributed ledger, while truly fine-grained details of bilateral or limited multilateral transactions are not recorded as transactions on the distributed ledger. The disadvantage is that there is a centralised system.

3.5.3.1 Lightning Network

The lightning network is the earliest scheme to form a payment network through the payment channel under the chain and improve the transaction throughput of the blockchain. It consists of a blockchain-based downlink transport network that works at the P2P level, and its availability depends on the creation of a two-way payment channel through which users can conduct seamless cryptocurrency transactions. To create a payment channel, both parties need to set up a multi-signature wallet and store some funds that can only be accessed if both parties provide private keys. After the two sides decide to open a payment channel, they can transfer money back and forth in their wallets. Although the process of establishing a payment channel involves transactions on the chain, all transactions that take place within the channel are on the chain and therefore do not require a global consensus. As a result, these trades can be executed quickly through smart contracts, allowing for higher TPS while paying lower fees.

However, there are some limitations of Lightning networks. If the receiver of both parties are not online, Lightning online payment cannot be made. In order to ensure the security of funds, it is necessary to monitor the payment channel regularly. Lightning networks are not suitable for large payments, because they rely on a large number of multi-signature wallets (basically Shared wallets), so they probably do not have enough balance to act as intermediaries for large payments. Creating and closing payment channels involves on-chain transactions that require manual operation and may incur high transaction costs.

3.5.3.2 Raiden Network

Model based on Ethernet, Raiden network reference the structure of the Lightning network. Since Raiden Network is a complementary network, it users a channel to deal with a number of deals, some of the encryption algorithm is then used to record and verify the actual transaction data under the chain. Finally, when the Channel is shut down, the transaction data is shut down. Actual cryptocurrency transactions and authentication are carried into the blockchain. In this way, the actual number of transactions on the blockchain will be reduced and transaction costs will be reduced and accelerated.

It works like the bar tab, because you only pay the total amount to the bar at the end of the day, instead of going through the entire payment process every time you buy a drink. Each bar tab is called a channel.

Any particular channel is one-to-one (for example, Alice to Bob) and the channels can be linked together to form a network so that users can

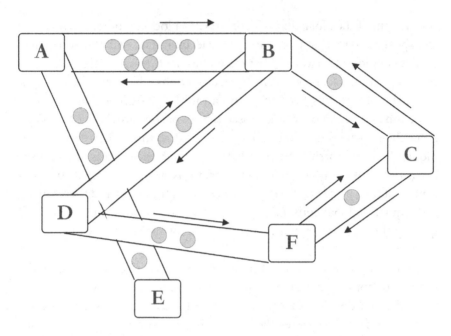

FIGURE 3.6   Process of Raiden Network.

pay anyone in the network. Figure 3.6 shows that even if F has only channel A, anyone in the network can pay F through the channel interaction
associated with A.

Since only two participants can receive deposits in the payment channel's
smart contracts, payment channel transfers are not affected by double-spend
attacks, making them as secure as transactions on the chain.

3.5.4 Cross-Chain Technology

Cross-chain is the technology to solve the problem of the interaction
between the chain and chain. The process can be divided into two stages:
assets on A chain of locking phase and the corresponding assets on the
chain B unlock stage. The main challenges are how to ensure that the asset
on chain A is locked, how to determine the asset on chain B is unlocked,
and how to guarantee the atomicity of asset locking and unlocking
between chain A and B, that is, the corresponding asset between two
chains either locks and unlocks successfully or locks and unlocks fail. For
the above challenges, different cross-chain technologies were proposed,
mainly including four categories.

3.5.4.1 Multi-Centre Witness

The Witness mechanism uses witness to guarantee the locking and unlocking of assets in different chains. The multi-signature script in the blockchain script is mainly used to realise the two-way exchange between the chains. The specific process is as follows: the user transfers the asset of chain A to the multi-signature script address of several witnesses for locking, and the witnesses release the corresponding asset to the address of the user in chain B after confirmation. This technology is applied in Byteball and DagCoin.

3.5.4.2 Side Chain/Relay Technology

The side chain is based on anchoring some kind of general certificate on the original chain, just like the dollar anchoring to gold. Sidechains are connected to various chains, while other blockchains can exist independently.

The representative of side chain technology is BTC Relay. It is considered the first side chain on the blockchain. BTC Relay connected the Ethereum network to the bitcoin network by using Ethereum's smart contracts, allowing users to verify bitcoin transactions on Ethereum. It creates a smaller version of the bitcoin blockchain through Ethereum's smart contracts, which require access to bitcoins' network data, making decentralisation difficult. The specific process is as follows:

a. Alice and Bob use the smart contract to conduct transactions. Alice users BTC coin to exchange Bob's ETH coin, and Bob sends his ETH coin to the smart contract;

b. Alice sends BTC coins to Bob's address.

c. Alice generates the SPV certificate through the transaction information of bitcoin and inputs the certificate into the contract in the ETH system;

d. After the contract is triggered, confirm the SPV certificate, and then release Bob's ETH coin to Alice's address before.

In addition, another typical implementation is Cosmos. It is a heterogeneous network developed by the Tendermint team that supports cross-chain interaction. Cosmos adopts the Tendermint consensus algorithm, which is similar to the practical Byzantine fault-tolerant consensus engine

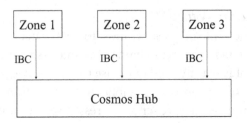

FIGURE 3.7   Structure on cosmos relay network.

with high performance, consistency, and under its strict bifurcated lia-bility system, can prevent malicious participants from making improper operations.

The central and individual Spaces of the Cosmos network can be com-municated through the blockchain communication (IBC) protocol, which is specific to the blockchain network, similar to the UDP or TCP network protocols, as shown in Figure 3.7. Tokens can be transferred safely and quickly from one space to another without the need for exchange liquidity. Instead, all transfers of tokens within the space go through the Cosmos centre, which records the total number of tokens held per space. This cen-tre separates each space from the other fault Spaces. Because everyone can connect the new space to the Cosmos centre, Cosmos is also compatible with future blockchains.

3.5.4.3 Hash Locking

Hash locking works in the same way as HTLC in Lightning networks. By using Hash preimage as secret and conditional payment, the atomicity of different transactions can be guaranteed without the participation of trusted third parties, so as to realise fair cross-chain exchange.

As shown in Figure 3.8, the process of cross-chain atom exchange is as follows:

a. A generates random number r and calculates its Hash value h, then send h to B.

b. A and Block up the assets for exchange successively by using HTLC. The locking time of A shall be longer than that of B, that is, T1 < T2. From the perspective of A, in time T1, B can obtain the asset locked by A through public image r, otherwise, A can redeem its asset. From

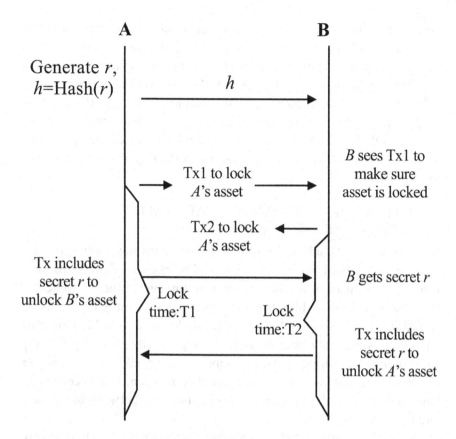

FIGURE 3.8   Process of cross-chain atomic swap.

the perspective of B, in time T2, A can obtain the asset locked by B through public image r, otherwise, B can redeem its asset.

c. A obtains the locked assets of B by publishing the preimage r. Meanwhile, B obtains secret r and obtains the locked assets of A on another chain by publishing r.

3.5.4.4 Distributed Private Key Control Technology

Private assets are mapped to the blockchain of built-in asset templates based on protocols through distributed private key generation and control technology, and new assets are created based on the deployment of new smart contracts which based on cross-chain transaction information. When a registered asset is transferred from the original chain to the cross-chain, the cross-chain node will issue corresponding tokens of equivalent value to the user in the existing contract. In order to ensure that the original chain assets can still trade with each other across the chain, the operation of realising and unlocking distributed control management is called lock-in and lock-out. Lock-in is the process of implementing distributed control management and asset mapping for all digital assets controlled by keys. The decentralised network needs to be entrusted with the user's private key, and the user holds the private key of the agent asset across the chain. When unlocked, control of the digital asset is returned to the owner.

3.6 SIMILARITIES BETWEEN BIG DATA AND BLOCKCHAIN TECHNOLOGY

Big data and blockchain technologies are constantly developing. There is a common keyword between big data and blockchain: distributed, representing a shift from the monopoly of technology authority to decentralisation. Some may think the two technologies are mutually exclusive. In fact, they are two complementary technologies. Like other emerging technologies, big data and blockchain are gradually changing the way some industries operate. What will happen when these two technologies are applied simultaneously? To answer this question, it is necessary to better understand the differences and connections between blockchain and big data.

The main similarities between big data and blockchain technology are as follows:

Distributed database: Due to the massive and fast-growing storage needs of big data to deal with, more and more distributed storage technologies have emerged. Hadoop (White, 2012), Spark (Zaharia, Chowdhury, Franklin, Shenker, & Stoica, 2010), MapReduce (Dean & Ghemawat, 2008), SAS, and Rapid Miner offer flexibility, and scalability performance to improve the storage capacity and the analytic process (Oussous, Benjelloun, Lahcen, & Belfkih, 2018; Tsai, Lai, Chao, & Vasilakos, 2015). Blockchain technology calculates and records data together through multiple nodes participating in the calculation in the network. From this point of view, blockchain technology is also a specific database technology.

Distributed Computing: The analysis of big data needs huge distributed computing power. Fault-tolerance, security, and access control are the critical requirements of big data technology (Dean & Ghemawat, 2008). The consensus mechanism of blockchain is to generate and update data through an algorithm. These three requirements are also needed by blockchain technology.

Serving the economy and society: Behind big data and blockchain technologies are urgent economic and social needs. The more centralised the application technology, the more complex the system will be, and the more difficult the implementation will be. The cost of communication and management is also getting higher and higher. The emergence of such distributed systems is from the needs of economic society.

3.7 DIFFERENCES BETWEEN BIG DATA AND BLOCKCHAIN TECHNOLOGIES

There are also many differences between big data and blockchain technology. As early as 1980, Alvin Toffler, a famous futurist, praised 'big data' as 'the colorful movement of the third wave' in his book *The Third Wave*. In October 2008, Satoshi Nakamoto described an electronic cash system called Bitcoin based on blockchain technology in his paper Bitcoin: a peer-to-peer electronic cash system (Nakamoto, 2008). As shown in Table 3.2, in big data, most of the data is unstructured, while data of blockchain is structured due to its special structure. What's more, big data sets are large and complex enough while the data that blockchain can carry now is limited, far from the big data standard. The blockchain system itself is a database, and the main purpose of big data is to deeply analyse and mine data. In terms of security and anonymity, big data is not as good as blockchain technology.

3.8 CHAPTER SUMMARY

Blockchain technology can be used in big data, and the technology ecology of big data flourishes. No software can solve all the problems. It can solve the problems only in a range, even Spark, Flink, etc. In the context

TABLE 3.2 Differences between Blockchain and Big Data

	Big Data	**Blockchain**
Appear time	1980	2008
Data structure	Mostly unstructured	Structured
Data size	Huge	Restricted
Purpose of data collection	Analysis and mining	Database
Security	Vulnerable to attack	Difficult to tamper with
Anonymity	Weak	Strong

of emphasising transparency and security, blockchain has its place. The use of blockchain technology on big data systems can prevent data from being added, modified, and deleted at will. Of course, the time and data magnitude are limited.

Taking time and data volume as the axis, the current big data engine is generally good at processing data. Blockchain can be a good supplement. For example, the centralization of big data is not secure enough. By adding blockchain, historical data cannot be tampered with. Yes, we can Hash the big data, add a timestamp, and store it on the blockchain. At some point in the future, when we need to verify the authenticity of the original data, we can do the same Hash processing on the corresponding data. If the answer is the same, it means that the data has not been tampered with. Or, only the aggregated data and results are processed. In this way, only incremental data processing needs to be processed, and the corresponding data magnitude and throughput level may be processed by today's blockchain or improved systems.

This chapter describes some of the key technologies of big data, the history of blockchain technology, and more. The types of blockchain types include public, private and consortium chains. Finally, some sections on the scalability of the blockchain are introduced. By combining big data and blockchain, the data in the blockchain can be made more valuable, and the predictive analysis of big data can be implemented into actions. They will all be the cornerstones of the digital economy.

REFERENCES

Androulaki, E., Barger, A., Bortnikov, V., Cachin, C., Christidis, K., De Caro, A., . . ., Manevich, Y. (2018). Hyperledger fabric: a distributed operating system for permissioned blockchains. Proceedings of the Thirteenth EuroSys Conference, ACM.

Buterin, V. (2014). Ethereum: *A next-generation smart contract and decentralized application platform*. Retrieved from https://github. com/ethereum/wiki/wiki/% 5BEnglish% 5D-White-Paper 7.

Dean, J., & Ghemawat, S. (2008). MapReduce: simplified data processing on large clusters. *Communications of the ACM, 51*(1), 107–113.

Nakamoto, S. (2008). Bitcoin: A peer-to-peer electronic cash system.

Oussous, A., Benjelloun, F.-Z., Lahcen, A. A., & Belfkih, S. (2018). Big Data technologies: A survey. *Journal of King Saud University-Computer and Information Sciences, 30*(4): 431–448.

Tsai, C.-W., Lai, C.-F., Chao, H.-C., & Vasilakos, A. V. (2015). Big data analytics: a survey. *Journal of Big Data, 2*(1), 21.

White, T. (2012). *Hadoop: The definitive guide*. O'Reilly Media, Inc. Sevastopol, California.

Zaharia, M., Chowdhury, M., Franklin, M. J., Shenker, S., & Stoica, I. (2010). Spark: Cluster computing with working sets. *HotCloud, 10*(10–10), 95.

Zheng, Z., Xie, S., Dai, H.-N., Chen, X., & Wang, H. (2018). Blockchain challenges and opportunities: A survey. *International Journal of Web and Grid Services, 14*(4), 352–375.

CHAPTER 4

Convergence of Blockchain and Big Data

4.1 THE COMMERCIAL VALUE OF BLOCKCHAIN

The essence of blockchain is to use the information technology to build the basis of business rules and provide a new business environment and order. Therefore, in this new business environment, organisations that identify with the new business order can stand out as new business leaders without many constraints of the original competitive environment, resources, and status. What they need to do is to develop new business solutions and build new business networks for customers on top of the blockchain technology framework. It is conceivable that blockchain offers a huge opportunity to disrupt the existing market order and advantages.

In the words of management, blockchain technology opens up a brand new organisational competition field. In fact, we can think that automation and intelligentisation provide the productivity foundation of digital business, while blockchain provides the digital material foundation of business relations or production relations. Without productive relations, the development of productive forces are limited. For example, such important business processes as the supply chain or Procure-to-Pay can be fully automatic and intelligent processing. However, if the business process chain or the parties on the network do not establish the basic relationship of trust through technology, the process still needs to be promoted through various administrative means such as personnel

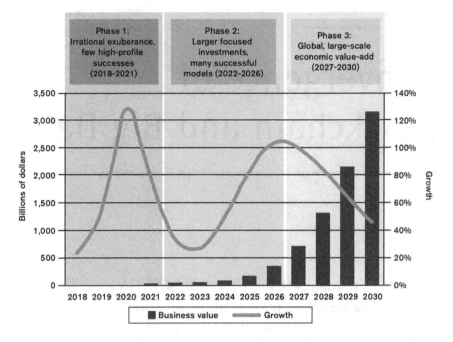

FIGURE 4.1   Gardner's prediction of blockchain business value highlights three stages of blockchain development.

signature, meeting, and so on. No amount of automation and intelligence is enough to make the expected real-time, concurrent business transactions impossible. This is the business value and opportunity of blockchain.

The World Trade Organization (WTO) has released a report on the impact of blockchain technology on international trade. As shown in Figure 4.1, according to the report's research, the global commercial value of blockchain will reach nearly $3 trillion by 2030.

Blockchain and International Trade: Opportunities, Challenges, and Implications for International Trade Cooperation analysed the problems and challenges that must be considered before blockchain is applied in various fields. The report covered research on the impact of blockchain technology on trade finance, customs clearance, logistics, and transportation. Research showed that blockchain has the potential to significantly reduce trade costs in areas including financial intermediation, exchange rate costs, and coordination by improving transparency and facilitating process automation.

While the decentralised and distributed nature of blockchains and the use of encryption technology make them highly resilient compared to traditional databases, they can also be affected by traditional security challenges.

The report highlighted the importance of developing a multi-stakeholder approach to finding appropriate use cases in the cross-border trade. According to the WTO, blockchain requires a framework that ensures network interoperability and provides a clear legal status for blockchain transactions across jurisdictions. The report concluded that blockchain can make international trade smarter, but smart trade requires the standardisation of intelligence, which can only be achieved through cooperation. If we can successfully create an ecosystem conducive to the broader development of blockchain, then in 10–15 years, international trade is likely to change fundamentally.

4.1.1 TCP/IP

If we look back at the development history and network structure of Internet technology and compare the current blockchain technology with the increasingly hot value interconnection concept, we can find that blockchain technology is indeed likely to become the future TCP/IP of value Internet.

Introduced in 1972, TCP/IP first gained attraction in a single-use case: as the basis for e-mail among the researchers on ARPAnet, the U.S. Department of Defense precursor to the commercial internet. Before TCP/IP, telecommunication architecture was based on 'circuit switching', in which connections between two parties or machines had to be pre-established and sustained throughout an exchange. To ensure that any two nodes could communicate, telecom service providers and equipment manufacturers had invested billions in building dedicated lines.

TCP/IP turned that model on its head. The new protocol transmitted information by digitising it and breaking it up into very small packets, each including address information. Once released into the network, the packets could take any route to the recipient. Smart sending and receiving nodes at the network's edges could disassemble and reassemble the packets and interpret the encoded data. There was no need for dedicated private lines or massive infrastructure. TCP/IP created an open, shared public network without any central authority or party responsible for its maintenance and improvement.

Traditional telecommunications and computing sectors looked on TCP/IP with scepticism. Few imagined that robust data, messaging, voice, and video connections could be established on the new architecture or that the associated system could be secured and scaled up. But during the late 1980s and 1990s, a growing number of firms, such as Sun, NeXT, Hewlett-Packard, and Silicon Graphics, used TCP/IP, in part to create localised private networks within organisations. To do so, they developed building blocks and tools that broadened its use beyond e-mail, gradually replacing more-traditional local network technologies and standards. As organisations adopted these building blocks and tools, they saw dramatic gains in productivity. TCP/IP burst into broad public use with the advent of the World Wide Web in the mid-1990s. New technology companies quickly emerged to provide the 'plumbing' – the hardware, software, and services needed to connect to the now-public network and exchange information. Netscape commercialised browsers, web servers, and other tools and components that aided the development and adoption of internet services and applications. Sun drove the development of Java, the application-programming language. As the information on the web grew exponentially, Infoseek, Excite, AltaVista, and Yahoo were born to guide users around it.

Once this basic infrastructure gained critical mass, a new generation of companies took advantage of low-cost connectivity by creating internet services that were compelling substitutes for existing businesses. CNET moved news online. Amazon offered more books for sale than any bookshop. Priceline and Expedia made it easier to buy airline tickets and brought unprecedented transparency to the process. The ability of these newcomers to get extensive reach at relatively low cost puts significant pressure on traditional businesses like newspapers and brick-and-mortar retailers. Relying on broad internet connectivity, the next wave of companies created novel, transformative applications that fundamentally changed the way businesses created and captured value. These companies were built on a new peer-to-peer architecture and generated value by coordinating distributed networks of users. Think of how eBay changed online retail through auctions, Napster changed the music industry, Skype changed telecommunications, and Google, which exploited user-generated links to provide more relevant results, changed web search. Ultimately, it took more than 30 years for TCP/IP to move through all the phases – single-use, localised use, substitution, and transformation – and reshape the economy. Today more than half the world's most valuable public companies have internet-driven, platform-based business models. The very foundations of our economy have changed. Physical scale and unique intellectual property no longer confer unbeatable advantages; increasingly, the economic leaders are enterprises that act as 'keystones', proactively organising, influencing, and coordinating widespread networks of communities, users, and organisations.

Blockchain – a peer-to-peer network that sits on top of the internet – was introduced in October 2008 as part of a proposal for bitcoin, a virtual currency system that eschewed a central authority for issuing currency, transferring ownership, and confirming transactions. Bitcoin was the first application of blockchain technology.

The parallels between blockchain and TCP/IP are clear. Just as e-mail enabled bilateral messaging, bitcoin enables bilateral financial transactions. The development and maintenance of the blockchain are open, distributed, and shared – just like TCP/IP's. A team of volunteers around the world maintains the core software. Moreover, just like e-mail, bitcoin first caught on with an enthusiastic but relatively small community. TCP/IP unlocked new economic value by dramatically lowering the cost of connections. Similarly, blockchain could dramatically reduce the cost of transactions. It has the potential to become the system of record for all transactions. If that happens, the economy will once again undergo a radical shift, as new, blockchain-based sources of influence and control emerge (Iansiti & Lakhani, 2017).

4.1.2 Smart Assets for the Society

Blockchain can be used for the registration, storage, and transaction of any digital asset, including tangible assets (physical assets) and intangible assets (votes, concepts, credits, ideas, health data, and information) in various fields such as finance, economy, and currency. For a variety of different types and levels of industry, the application provides connection and integration.

Smart assets generally refer to all tradable proprietary assets based on the blockchain model. These assets may be real assets in the physical world, such as houses, cars, bicycles, or computers, or intangible assets such as stocks, savings, or copyrights (such as books, music, paintings, and digital art). Any asset can be registered in the blockchain, and its ownership is owned by the person controlling the private key. The owner can sell the asset by transferring the private key or the asset to another party.

Extensive construction of decentralised asset management systems that do not require the trust of third parties and control of assets through cryptography. This may be able to obtain a great application in the scope of property law, by recording the property itself to greatly simplify the management of asset ownership. Automatically executed smart contract code is bound to the bottom of the code and cannot be stripped away, which cannot prevent the occurrence of the property right transaction preset by the code. Smart contracts are characterised by two parties agreeing to do something or not agreeing to do something without having to trust each other. In fact, smart contracts work this way mainly because of three factors: autonomy, self-sufficiency, and decentralisation. First, autonomy means that the contract is automatically executed as soon as it is started, without any intervention by its originator. Second, smart contracts can acquire resources in their own way, that is, by providing services or issuing assets to obtain funds that can be used when needed; Finally, smart contracts are decentralised, that is, they do not depend on a single centralised server but are distributed and run automatically through network nodes.

4.1.3 Docking Machine Economy

The Internet of Things is built on the Internet, the network that connects everything together. 'Things' in IoT means everything, which can be any ordinary physical object. As machines become more intelligent, the number of Internet-of-things devices and the value of their output will grow faster and faster, creating the need for a network of micropayments to connect and manage transactions between smart devices. A possible future scenario would be for the vending machine to notify an empty delivery truck to restock when it runs out of items. When the replenishment is complete, the vending machine automatically pays for the goods to the delivery truck. Blockchain technology can be perfectly applied to this scenario. Since the trust between machines cannot be handled, the trust mechanism brought by the blockchain technology to the third party can just make up for the lack of trust between machines. All this is not pure fantasy. IBM and Samsung recently came up with an application that would allow household appliances such as dishwashers to issue commands to detergent suppliers by executing smart contracts. Smart contracts give the device the ability to pay for orders, receive payment confirmation messages and shipping messages from the retailer, and notify the owner via ringtone alerts.

In a decentralised Internet of things, blockchain is the infrastructure that facilitates collaboration between transaction processing and interacting devices. Each blockchain manages its own behaviour and plays its own role, thus forming a 'decentralized autonomous Internet of things'. Economic behaviour in the future may not only be limited to people or organisations but also to machines. Blockchain technology will open the era of the machine economy.

The future Internet of things will be an important source of big data. How to improve the quality of big data in the Internet of things and how to effectively screen, integrate, and process big data in the Internet of things is the key. The blockchain has the ability to play a huge role. The current Internet of things is still passive operation and data generation, the future further machine economy will be artificial intelligence. Where artificial intelligence goes beyond the Internet of things is that it can carry out active control and information screening, which greatly optimises the generation of basic data for big data, rather than collecting data indiscriminately like the Internet of things sensors. It can be said that artificial intelligence is the upgrade of the Internet of things. Or rather, a significant part of the traditional Internet of things will sooner or later be replaced by artificial intelligence. As can be expected, unarrived Artificial intelligence (AI) will become an important data source for big data. However, the high-quality information and services of artificial intelligence need to transfer the value generated by itself through the value-based Internet built by the blockchain technology more, and it will be more suitable for the blockchain network in terms of technology, and can even participate in various commercial operations of the value Internet with an independent identity. The prospect of how big data and other intelligent assets generated and controlled by artificial intelligence will spread and be traded on the blockchain value. Internet is likely to be far beyond the imagination of humans today.

4.1.4 Optimise the Social Structure

Blockchain is the essence of a mass collaboration tool. Its influence is not confined to the individual, and it will change the way we all cooperate. In his book out of control: the ultimate destiny and end of humanity, Kevin Kelly, a prominent sociologist, discusses how human society and science and technology will evolve. He summarised the evolution of industrial society as one based on mechanical logic, and the evolution of information society as one based on biological logic. This theory of evolution, based on biological logic, can be summed up in three words: distributed, decentralised, and self-organising. The application of this idea in technology has enabled us to make great progress in such technical fields as communication networks. With the help of blockchain technology, we can practice these ideas in real social organisations. Decentralised Autonomous Organisation (DAO), Decentralised Autonomous Corporation (DAC), and Decentralised Autonomous Society (DAS) can solve a considerable number of practical problems to a large extent.

Voting is still one of the most common ways to solve problems in the decision-making process, especially when it comes to some public decisions, and it provides equal opportunities for everyone. Although electronic voting systems are used everywhere in the world, it still takes hours of manual verification. Even in countries with long voting traditions, the potential for fraud remains. If the entire voting process is recorded on the distributed ledger of the blockchain, its tamper-proof and truth-free nature will make the results more convincing. We can vote on specific issues, but decisions without our assets don't support an organisation's operations. Daos are entities with internal assets that are built to run autonomously on a decentralised platform. Strictly speaking, DAC is a form of DAO. The term was first coined by Daniel Larimer, who has always insisted that DAC pay dividends. That is, DAC has the concept of shares and can be bought and traded in a way that allows the holder to continue to enjoy the success of DAC. With the maturity of DAO and DAC, the whole society will eventually form DAS, and human civilisation will enter a new stage.

Blockchain society is a form of DAS, which refers to the realisation of traditional services provided by the government and social management institutions as well as more and brand new social management and services in a decentralised, more convenient, more effective, and more personalised way through blockchain technology. The government and social institutions can make use of the advantages of blockchain technology to publicly store social files for easy access and further social management.

Another important implication of the DAS is personalisation. Government administration and services can be customised according to individual needs from a single unified model. For example, a resident may have to pay more for better garbage service, while his neighbour may have to pay for a better school. It is possible for the 'government on the blockchain' to represent the public opinion more truly, understand the demand of public opinion more keenly, and make policy and regulation adjustments more deftly and nimbly to optimise the social structure, improve social governance, and promote social progress. The emergence of DAS puts forward the thinking of how to opti-mise the social governance structure for the government. How the framework of human rights and obligations will change, and what governance structure will emerge, is very exciting.

With the promotion of blockchain, the concepts of DAO, DAC, and DAS will be increasingly respected by knowledgeable people. The way of scien-tific and technological innovation is bound to gradually transform from traditional engineering team to individual. In a mature distributed autono-mous system, there is no concept of 'authority', and anyone can express their views and ideas to others without interference. As long as the solu-tion is smart and logical, enough support will be available, and all services will be global. Then, in this process, government management and social operation will be big data in a comprehensive way, and social big data will emerge as The Times require, and become an indispensable part of human life. Blockchain technology will be the most important driving force.

4.2 WHAT CHANGES CAN BLOCKCHAIN BRING?

In the face of the surging tide of digitalisation, as early as 2008, Chris Anderson, editor-in-chief of Wired magazine, believed that big data would profoundly change the way humans explore the world. He even thought that quantum mechanics was divorced from reality and the theory was over. As long as there was a lot of data, applied mathematics could be used as a tool to explore the world. Anderson is right that big data matters. What's really wrong is that behind his claim, his perception of the world remains Newtonian, like most people's. The world is mechanical and absolute, and motion can be calculated precisely. Everything has a cause and effect. Cause and effect correspond, cause and effect are continuous, and future consequences can be predicted. In the same way, the cause can be derived from the result, and the original only cause can be pushed for-ward. So, the world is continuous, things are linear, and trajectories are continuous, based on causal drives.

In big data technology, correlation replaces causality, while mash-ups replace precision. In his book *Reinventing Capitalism in the Age of Big Data*, Viktor Mayer-Schönberger argued that we don't have to know what's behind the phenomenon, but let the data speak for itself. He also said that correlation can help us better understand the world and believed that prediction based on correlation analysis is the core of big data. By finding 'correlations' and monitoring them, we can predict the future.

The value of big data lies in the integration of multi-source data. Due to the privacy, complexity, asymmetric supply, and demand of data, the current data circulation has seriously restricted the development of the value of big data in society. The problems of data opening, sharing, and privacy protection are vital bottlenecks in the development of big data. Considering some characteristics of blockchains, such as transparency, security, auditability, and privacy, can be complementary to big data, many start-ups, enterprises, and governments are exploring their applications in the supply chain, electronic health records, voting, energy supply, ownership management, and protection of critical civilian infrastructure. Blockchain could also upend a number of complex intermediate functions in the industry: identity and reputation, moving value (payments and remittances), storing value (savings), lending and borrowing (credit), trading value (marketplaces like stock exchanges), insurance and risk management, and audit and tax functions. Figure 4.2 depicts a proposal to cover a secure lifecycle of a big data ecosystem, including the different sets of phases and how they relate to each other Moreno, Serrano, Fernandez, and Fernández-Medina (2020).

After the craze in recent years, the development of big data has entered a new stage: first, with the continuous emergence of new technologies and new hot spots, the attention of big data has gradually declined, hype and investment began to cool down, and the impetuous industry gradually dissipated; second, after the initial rapid advance, big data applications that can achieve simple and rapid results have made breakthroughs, and

Big Data Lifecycle

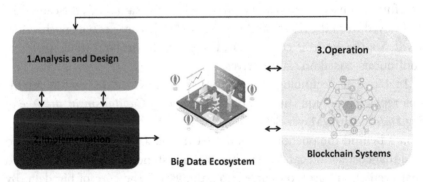

FIGURE 4.2   A lifecycle for a big data ecosystem.

the time period for further progress has begun to lengthen. Third, some technical and business logic constraints faced by big data have begun to block the rapid development of big data in a substantial way, so it is urgent to remove these obstacles quickly and effectively.

There are two types of obstacles to the development of big data. One is the obstacles related to technology, such as basic data collection, processing speed, storage space, analysis technology, and so on, the original related technology will naturally be unable to cope with the continuous increase in mass data. More importantly, in the face of low-value data, which accounts for a large proportion, is there only one way out? Is there a more efficient way to expand capacity while improving the ability to filter data before processing? The other kind of substantive obstacle comes mainly from business logic, in the face of a data island, even if there is no good ability to do. How can the value of shared data be highlighted and the barriers of data silos be broken down? What may be faced here is not only the problem of the business logic of big data itself but also the need to consider whether the current social organisation form and the use mode of data have become the shackles of the development of big data. Blockchain technology has emerged in the past 2 years. Due to its distinctive characteristics and advantages, it has not only become an eye-catching new hotspot but also provided a new solution for many industrial problems and a new possibility for promoting the development of the sharing society. So, can big data get the help of blockchain technology, overcome a series of obstacles it encountered, and achieve a new round of substantial development?

Blockchain and big data technology have evolved step by step along with human society. Although the technology of big data is developing, big data risk control is not perfect, and there are still insufficient issues such as data silos, data low-quality, and data leakage. The underlying logic of blockchain is decentralisation, openness, and transparency. Blockchain technology can solve the trust problem in the Internet environment, so as to promote the rapid development of big data and the digital economy. After the online big data of the Internet encountered the blockchain, it was endorsed by strong trust, which inspired more data industries to emerge. By using smart contracts, some common big data scenarios in social life can be combined with blockchain technology to build a new generation of applications. They will focus on building trust, accountability, and transparency while simplifying business processes and legal constraints. In this section, we will analyse some potential benefits of combining blockchain with big data.

4.2.1 Security and Privacy

Blockchain technology ensures big data security and privacy through its decentralised system. Most of the data is stored in centralised servers, which can lead to leakage and loss of data. They are often targeted by cyber attackers. Blockchains decentralise control over data, making it a daunting task for cybercriminals to access and manipulate data on a massive scale. In addition, the transaction data on the blockchain, including the transaction address, amount, and transaction time, are all open and transparent. But the identity of the owner of the transaction address is anonymous. Through the encryption of blockchain technology, the user's identity and user data can be separated through the encryption algorithm.

The combination of blockchain and big data is most widely used in healthcare. The healthcare industry must ensure the security, privacy, and integrity of healthcare data. This is the demand for a sound and secure data management system. According to an EMC report researched and analysed by IDC, healthcare accounts for a significant proportion of data in the digital world. After analysis, André Gonçalves et al. (2016) found that data growth in healthcare will be faster than the rest of the digital universe. In terms of the health care industry, by the end of 2011, the global health care data storage has reached 150 EB (1 EB=1018 bytes), mainly in the form of electronic health records. It is predicted that the volume of global health care data will escalate to 35 ZB (1 ZB=1021 bytes) in 2020 (Raghupathi & Raghupathi, 2014). However, most potential value creation is still in the early stages because predictive modelling and simulation techniques for analysing the entire medical data are not yet fully developed. Azaria et al. introduced MedRec (Azaria et al., 2016), which uses a permissioned blockchain network to give patients a comprehensive, immutable log, and easy access to their medical information across providers and treatment sites. By taking advantage of blockchain, MedRec manages authentication, confidentiality, and accountability – crucial considerations when handling sensitive information. Since the blockchain can perform asymmetric encryption, it allows for differential privacy. In this way, patients can share clinical records without having to share sensitive data.

4.2.2 Credibility and Transparency

Using blockchain technology as an intermediary, big data can provide data analysis for demanders through the automatic execution process of smart contracts. It reduces human intervention and redundancy through smart contracts. Through scanning and accurate analysis of all data, the blockchain network is combined with the automatic execution of smart contracts, which is unfamiliar but trusted by many parties. Xiaofeng Meng et al. (2018) designed a closed-loop analytical architecture based on Big Data and Blockchain in the Medical and Health Industry to ensure the quality of the decision. Big data and blockchain can combine together to ensure the mutual trust of data, realise transaction endorsement, and provide a guarantee for the final construction of asset exchange and value transactions in the digital economy world. The combination of blockchain and big data can also improve the transparency of the industry. For example, in the two aspects of auto finance and auto insurance, there are a lot of illegal businesses seeking large profits from customers. Improving industry transparency can effectively protect the rights and interests of consumers. Damiano Di Francesco Maesa et al. (2019) proposed a blockchain-based approach for the definition of auditable access control systems. Both the resource owner and the subject making the access request can easily detect inappropriate authorisation or access denial, thanks to publicly auditable evidence of misconduct.

4.2.3 Data Sharing

In the era of big data, data security issues not only contain the personal privacy protection issues but also include the issue of data analysis which aims to predict the people's status and behaviour. The data stored in the blockchain is structured and complete, which contributes to further analysis. Fedak (2018) asserted that blockchain not only makes big data even bigger but also contributes by making big data more secure and valuable as blockchained big data is structured and ready for big data analytics.

Zhuojie Huang (2019) showed that blockchain can ensure trust and improve data integrity among different entities in the cross-border logistics network. All entities in the cross-border supply chain will combine order data, location data, node-aware data, financial contract data, and transaction data in a distributed manner and agree on the level of detail of the share. A data analyst can use these real-time, traceable, better-integrated data for real-time analysis and optimisation to achieve a global optimisation model.

Through the distributed characteristics of blockchain, huge computing power can be obtained. Even in small organisations, data analysts can undertake a wide range of prediction and analysis tasks. These analysts can use the computing power of thousands of computers connected to the blockchain network as cloud-based services to analyse data.

4.2.4 Data Analysis

The blockchain has solved the security problem of data sharing to a certain extent. Using blockchain technology, big data gained from data research can be stored in the blockchain network. The project team will not repeat the data analysis that other teams have already performed and will not reuse the used data by mistake. In addition, the blockchain platform can help researchers monetise their work through the analysis results of transactions stored on the platform.

Healthcare is a typical multi-center scenario, and no one institution has all the data. As the demand for personal health management increases, various health service agencies hope to collect health information through medical data exchange and sharing (Chen et al., 2019). Such as the U.S. government's Blue Button Connector and Hong Kong's health system. But these applications still have problems in data sharing. Blockchain technology is a new technology, which can realise data sharing in a decentralised and transactional way. Blockchain technology can be used in the field of healthcare to achieve a delicate balance between privacy and the accessibility of electronic medical records (Dagher et al., 2018). As a combination of distributed storage, point-to-point transmission, consensus mechanism, and encryption algorithms, blockchain provides a solution for data sharing. The IBM report believes that in 2020, 56% of medical institutions worldwide will invest in blockchain technology. Healthcare is a relatively high-informatisation industry, and its stock data is already large. Today, what the blockchain does is to break the data silos and give the data greater value. QI Xia et al. proposed MeDShare (Xia et al., 2017). This system addresses the issue of medical data sharing among medical big data custodians in a trustless environment. The system is blockchain-based and provides data provenance, auditing, and control for shared medical data in cloud repositories among big data entities. By implementing MeDShare, cloud service providers and other data guardians will be able to share medical data with entities such as research and medical institutions. Aiqing Zhang and Lin (2018) proposed a blockchain-based secure and privacy-preserving PHI sharing (BSPP) scheme for diagnosis improvements in Electronic health systems. Simon Lebech Cichosz et al. (2019) presented an approach for a blockchain-based platform for sharing Diabetes Health Care Data. This method regards privacy issues, data sharing, and patients as the center of managing their own data.

Blockchain technology can also accelerate the research of genomic big data. In 2018, the number of genotyped people surpassed 10 million and is expected to grow to more than 100 million by 2021 (Khan & Mittelman, 2018). However, sequencing costs, data privacy concerns, regulatory restrictions, and technical challenges impede the growth of genomic data and hinder data sharing. Harvard Dennis Grishin et al. (2018) described one approach to overcoming these obstacles, using a combination of multiple technologies, named Nebula – a decentralised genomic data generation, sharing, and analysis platform. The Nebula blockchain is an Exonum-based blockchain through which the Nebula network will be governed, consent will be documented, and the data will be secured, so as to share genomic data better.

4.2.5 Protection of Data Sovereignty

At present, the use of most data is not controlled by its owners because there is no reliable way to record the way in which data is used and who records it. So there's almost no way to track or punish violators who use that data without limit. Blockchain can further standardise the use of big data and refine the scope of authorisation, so as to protect the relevant rights and interest of data. Uchi Ugobame Uchibeke, Schneider, Kassani, and Deters (2018) provided an architecture for access control management by using a decentralised security system based on hyperledger blockchain. In their Blockchain Role-Based Access Control Business Network (BRBACBN). The data are owned by the organisation, and the personnel working in the organisation are granted access to a subset of big data according to their roles in the organisation. Organisations use their keys or perform operations through users authorised by the organisation to assign roles to users. When users try to access data sets, the smart contracts or transactions verify that users have access to the data, thereby ensuring the rights of big data. Chao Lin et al. (2018) proposed the conceptual blockchain-based system (BSeIn) for remote mutual authentication with fine-grained access control. Only authorised participants can gain access to the 'original' context of the request message. The whole request process is executed by interacting with the smart contract.

4.2.6 Cost Reduction

Blockchain technology is a potential solution to reduce corporate costs. Blockchain technology solves the problem of trust and reliable value transfer at a very low cost, with anti-counterfeiting and anti-tampering features, and can build a more shared, transparent, open, reliable, and verifiable reliable system. When applying blockchain to existing systems, it is important to evaluate the cost reduction due to the introduction of blockchain (Sawa, 2019). Especially in banks, blockchain has the potential to save costs by reducing transaction and processing costs. Hossein Hassani et al. (2018) held that blockchain is disrupting the banking industry and contributing to the increased big data in banking. In 2018, the Citigroup identified that cost savings is the main value of blockchains in the immediate future. A report released by Santander, Spain's largest bank, shows that around 2020 if banks around the world use blockchain technology internally, it will save about $20 billion in annual costs. Capgemini, a consulting company, estimates that consumers can save up to $16 billion in banking and insurance fees each year through blockchain-based applications (Tapscott & Tapscott, 2017).

4.3 BLOCKCHAIN TECHNOLOGY RECONSTRUCTS BIG DATA INDUSTRY

There are still obvious problems in the development of the big data industry. Different data sources not only affect the effect of the data mining but also can conclude that the results of data analysis are misleading. However, due to the reproducibility of the data in the transaction process, the transaction intermediary is not trusted, which affects the willingness to share and trade. If the data is not traded or circulated, the generation, analysis, and utilisation of the data only stay in the closed environment, such an island of data will greatly reduce the value of the data. How to realise the value of big data under the premise of protecting data privacy is a big problem at present.

Blockchain technology can fully improve many elements of multiple links in the big data industry. It not only entrusts big data with true and reliable ownership identification, convenient transfer, and exchange methods but also ensures the high quality of data and provides perfect solutions for data security and privacy protection. Blockchain technology provides a solid foundation for data sharing transactions. Big data can be easily traced on the blockchain network, fully realising the value of data, and thus achieving a far more optimised social configuration and efficient utilisation under the control of economic laws. Smart contracts using blockchain may realise more granular data transaction patterns, such as entry transaction, credit transaction for post-payment, recharge transaction, authorisation scenario transaction, data exchange transaction, and so on, so as to change the current business model of big data trading. Relying on the blockchain system, we can establish a credit investigation mechanism for all users, and promote the construction of the whole social credit system to a higher level. The flow of data transactions desensitised by blockchain technology is conducive to breaking through the island of information and establishing the horizontal flow mechanism of data. The value transfer network based on the blockchain gradually promotes the formation of a data transaction scenario based on globalisation and establishes the big data industry that truly belongs to the whole society.

4.3.1 Circulation Environment for Trusted Data Asset

In the centralised data flow mode, the central node has the conditions and ability to copy and save all the flowing data, which is unfair to the data producers. Such pitfalls cannot be eliminated by promises alone and are a huge obstacle to the flow of data. The decentralised blockchain can eliminate the potential threat of central node copying data, which is conducive to establishing a trusted data asset circulation environment.

It is worth referring to Windhover's Windhover Principles for digital identity, trust, and data. It is a principled framework written in collaboration with public and private sector stakeholders to protect individual identity, trust, and access to shared public data on the Internet.

Principle 1: the right to the control of personal identity and personal data.

Principle 1 is intended to give individuals control over their digital identity certificates and personal data, not society, government or business. To build a digital society and strengthen the innovation of digital technology, the primary task should be to improve the management and implementation of privacy. For example, each person's id card information is shared by the government, banks, hospitals, and so on. If one organisation discloses it, the information is shared by the whole world, which violates principle 1.

Principle 2: transparent implementation and effective governance.

Principle 2 is intended to strengthen the management of personal privacy, improve regulatory legal auditing, and strengthen law enforcement. In order to meet principle 1, any organisation can only know a short-term or partial identity of an individual but cannot have permanent or full identity information. For example, hospitals can know health records but not financial records. In the age of big data, organisations want to link multiple pieces of information about a person. So we need principle 2.

Principle 3: ensure trust and privacy.

Principle 3 is intended to establish an effective autonomous identification system, which needs to deepen the protection mechanism of privacy, trust, security, governance, and accountability. Any security and protection mechanisms must be constantly improved when motivated impure people continue to attempt to gain access to the system. So, we need principle 3 again.

Principle 4: collaboration through open source.

Principle 4 is intended to embody these rules in an inclusive, open-source approach to building systems that allow people to trust such security mechanisms. Some blockchain system is open source, while some not. However, the operation mechanism of the blockchain technology itself ensures that only the person who has the data right really owns the data, which reaches the standard of a trustworthy system.

The ultimate goal of the Windhover Principles is that an individual's identity can be owned and controlled by himself. If each data individual is treated as a distributed autonomous organisation, this principle will also facilitate the establishment of a trusted data asset circulation environment. In the highly distributed and decentralised scenario in the future, blockchain will take charge of data asset management, transaction, payment, smart contract, and other businesses in global decentralised data circulation. Blockchain technology will also be applied to personal data control (such as OpenMustardSeed framework) and distributed data storage (such as MaidSafe). The future Internet data layer is likely to be built on the basis of blockchain, and superimpose network layer and application layer on it, becoming the next generation of Internet infrastructure platform. The future flow of data may be built on these new infrastructures.

4.3.2 Programmable Economy

As a new economic model based on automation and mathematical algorithms, Programmable Economy writes the execution process of transactions into an automated programmable language and guarantees the automaticity and integrity of transaction execution by forcing pre-implanted instructions to run by code. This will bring unprecedented technological innovation, greatly reduce transaction supervision costs at the execution level, and have huge application prospects in reducing fraud, fighting corruption, simplifying supply chain transactions and other opportunistic behaviours, which will be the development direction of the new economy in the future.

The smart contract of blockchain is a typical programmable technology, which can not only automatically realise the pre-set intelligent operation but also play a huge role in economic life by combining the real, tamper-proof, safe, and reliable features of the blockchain. Blockchain can optimise the transaction organisation form and effectively promote the improvement of economic and social operation efficiency.

The transformational power of technological innovation affects the change of transaction cost to varying degrees. It is under the condition of rapid changes in the cost structure, relying on wide area coverage of the Internet's strong support, the boundary of the entity in the smaller, the boundary of the virtual organisation in the larger, and presents the tendency of blur, open, and even disappear, cause alone run on blockchain of autonomous entities, such as distributed autonomous organisation and distributed autonomous companies, this is the new organisation which is formed by the body in the pursuit of economic efficiency.

From the perspective of history, the change of the boundaries of autonomous organisations will not only change the internal connection structure but also change the external connection state. The purposeful interaction behaviour will prompt the organisation to spontaneously evolve to a higher form, thus changing the connection structure and supervision mode of the whole social organisation. The transaction cost savings and trust reconstruction brought by blockchain improve not only the efficiency of social management but also social governance. Blockchain may eventually lead to a more just, orderly, and secure autonomous society. The smart contract and full programmable extensibility of blockchain make full preparations for the coming of the smart society in the future.

4.3.3 Anonymity

In a blockchain system, exchanges between nodes follow a fixed algorithm without trust. Therefore, the counterparty does not need to disclose its identity to gain trust, which is very helpful for the credit accumulation of the node. In computer science, anonymity is an alias that has no relevance. The so-called anonymity means that from the perspective of the attacker, it is impossible to associate any two interactions between the user and the system. In bitcoin, it is obvious that connections can be established between transactions because the user repeatedly uses the public key hash as the transaction identifier. So bitcoin is not anonymous. Blockchain technology is anonymous because it is not known who the actual holder of each address is. You can prove that the address is yours by signing the address. You can only sign the specified address if you have a private key to the bitcoin address. Make use of the technical advantages of blockchain to ensure the anonymity of the whole blockchain system, participate in transactions without identity endorsement, and accumulate an untameable credit record on the network.

4.3.4 Convenience of Payment

With the rise of mobile payments, it has become the norm to go out with your phone instead of your wallet. But across the globe, cross-border remittances are far from easy, and people still face high costs, time delays, and error-prone problems. According to the World Bank, global cross-border payments grew at an average annual rate of 5% to reach $601 billion in 2016, and China is expected to surpass Brazil as the third-largest payment region after the United States and the eurozone. However, cross-border remittances are now costly, with an average rate of 7.68% per remitter.

The remittance process of the Swift system is as follows. The first step is that after receiving the remittance demand, the institution should first conduct anti-money laundering verification and identity verification, collect funds and corresponding fees, and then begin to process the remitter's request. Second, in the transfer process, since not all banks have joined the Swift alliance, banks or remittance institutions have to use two channels to transfer cross-border funds: Swift members can use the Swift network, while non-members can only remit through the local agent bank. The third step is for the receiver to go to the bank or remittance agency after receiving the notice. In the fourth step, the bank or remittance agent authenticates the identity. Step five: the receiver receives the remittance in local currency. Finally, banks or money transfer agencies are sometimes required to submit reports to regulators, including transaction details, depending on local regulatory policies.

In fact, the entire Swift system was established in the 1970s, which was relatively efficient and fast in the technical background of that year, but it inevitably fell behind after the Internet information revolution. Blockchain technology can make transactions faster and cheaper than traditional trading systems. The global network based on the blockchain technology can realise remittance transfer in near real-time and still maintain the advantages of the original blockchain such as anonymity, traceability, and tamper-proof. However, the single transaction link of the blockchain network, without the participation of other agents and intermediaries, makes the global remittance cost close to the common transaction cost of the blockchain network. Whether it's transaction speed, transaction security, or transaction costs, the blockchain system has revolutionised long-established global remittance patterns. Indeed, when bitcoin's price soared to record highs in late 2016 and early 2017, there were rumours that it had become a conduit for global remittances to circumvent China's currency controls. The internet-based transaction process and dealmaking make a sharp contrast between the blockchain business model and the traditional banking business model such as remittance, which reflects huge advantages.

4.3.5 Irreversibility

Blockchain is a consensus realisation technology, through which all transactions of the whole network can be recorded and consensus can be witnessed by users of the blockchain. The contents of the information on the chain cannot be tampered with. This irreversibility is caused by the presence of multiple copies in the system that increases the cost of malicious tampering of the content.

When all the records are published, the problem of 'two tables cannot be measured' in real life is solved. The reason why the two tables are unmeasurable is that there is no center. The values of the two tables are different. There are multiple nodes on the blockchain, each with a table. When there are multiple tables, and the majority points to one time and the minority is subordinate to the majority, the viewer knows. Therefore, a problem to be solved by blockchain is that 'the minority is subordinate to the majority'. The existence of a minority may be errors in data generation or maliciously tampered content. In other words, if you want to tamper successfully, you have to change 51% of the copies (i.e. 51% of the attacks) in the bitcoin system from a minority to a majority. It is conceivable that the cost of tampering from technical difficulty, time consumption, personnel use is huge. The transaction information of the whole network is absolutely true and reliable, cannot be tampered with, will not be lost, this kind of thought is undoubtedly the strengthened version and upgraded version of all current credit supervision models. By combining blockchain with various existing credit evaluation channels and giving full play to the advantages of blockchain, solutions can be found for establishing a truly effective credit society model. Based on objective and real data, value exchange is possible.

4.4 CHALLENGES IN THE CONVERGENCE OF BLOCKCHAIN AND BIG DATA

This section studies the main challenges to be solved when applying blockchain technology to the field of big data. The birth time of blockchain is too short and the technical framework is not mature enough. Although blockchain can bring many benefits to big data management, there are still some noteworthy challenges. Compared with most of the other technologies, blockchain is still in the 'infant' stage, and there are some practical problems such as weak scalability, low efficiency, and high handling costs, which cannot meet the large-scale commercialisation of multi-domain distributed applications (DAPP). At the same time, due to key technologies such as smart contract, shard, cross-chain, and side chain, POS, DPOS, and other consensus mechanisms as well as economic incentive models are still in the trial stage. Blockchain technology still has many defects. Therefore, the integration of blockchain technology with big data is not trivial. Iansiti and Lakhani (2017) think the development of blockchain needs to face an unprecedented level of social complexity. They developed a framework that maps current blockchain applications against two contextual dimensions, dividing them into quadrants. As showed in Figure 4.3, each quadrant represents a stage of technology development. The higher the complexity, coordination, and novelty of projects, the more difficult it is for the new application of blockchain and big data to be implemented. Some of the identified challenges are presented in this section. Figure 4.4 illustrates the five representative challenges of the convergence of blockchain and big data.

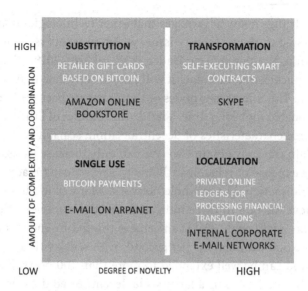

FIGURE 4.3 A framework for blockchain adoption.

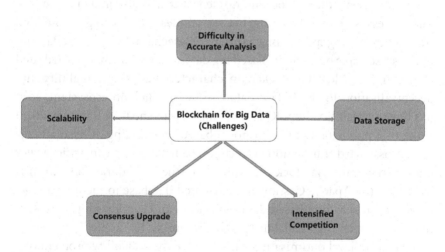

FIGURE 4.4 Representative challenges in the convergence of blockchain and big data.

4.4.1 Scalability

In big data, a lot of data needs to be processed and analysed. Therefore, data storage must support high transaction throughput and high scalability. Scalability is defined as the ability of a system, network, or process to expand its potential by handling increasing workloads. Although blockchain brings many advantages that other technologies don't have, it is still exposed to the scalability issue, which prevents real-time trading (Mengelkamp, Notheisen, Beer, Dauer, & Weinhardt, 2018). The larger the size of the blockchain, the longer it will take to copy data to new nodes on the network. This affects new nodes or those that are back online and have not been updated for a long time. Vitalik, the founder of Ethereum, thinks that the three characteristics of decentralisation, scalability, and security of blockchain can only obtain two. We can only increase transaction volume at the expense of reliability, that is to say, we can't reach consensus on every transaction on the whole network. Many blockchain networks try to achieve the best in three indicators through complex rule settings. Fabric (Androulaki et al., 2018) can achieve the end-to-end throughput of more than 3,500 transactions per second, with a delay time of less than 1 second, and can be well extended to more than 100 peers. BigchainDB (McConaghy et al., 2016) is a large-scale decentralised database. It introduced a concept called the blockchain pipeline, which is the key to achieve scalability when adding blockchain-like features to distributed databases. The process is mainly the voting between nodes, which can generate high transaction throughput for BigchainDB. HBasechainDB (Sahoo & Baruah, 2018) is a scalable blockchain-based big data storage system for distributed computing. It adds the blockchain characteristics of immutability and decentralisation to the HBase database in the Hadoop ecosystem, so it has linear scalability. RapidChain (Zamani, Movahedi, & Raykova, 2018) is the first public blockchain protocol based on sharding. It used an efficient cross-shard transaction verification technique and can achieve very high throughputs via block pipelining. Mystiko (Bandara et al., 2018) is built over the Apache Cassandra distributed database to incorporate big data. It used sharding-based data replication and supports high transaction throughput, high scalability, high availability.

Algorithm level optimisation cannot solve the scalability problem of a large-scale decentralised system. Some schemes implemented under the chain are contrary to the idea of blockchain decentralisation. Therefore, most of the leading blockchain projects above adopt a scalable method like sharding. However, these scalable methods will bring some security problems. Since participants cannot download and verify the history of the entire slice, they cannot be sure that the results they interact with have been written to the block. Therefore, we should continue to study the blockchain solution for big data and find a more complete one.

4.4.2 Difficulty in Accurate Analysis

With the rapid development of the application of blockchain technology, the data scale will become larger and larger. The data fusion of blockchain in different business scenarios will further expand the data scale and richness. Although anonymity and privacy protection are one of the main characteristics of blockchain, it also makes it extremely difficult for researchers to obtain valuable information from blockchain data sets. The key and difficult point of on-chain data analysis is mining the relationship between accounts and addresses. The more anonymous the blockchain data set is, the more difficult it is for accurate marketing to individuals. Researchers can only get general rules from these data, but it is difficult to accurately predict the future behaviour and results of individuals. The combination of blockchain and big data forms a very complex network. With the anonymity of blockchain, it is very difficult to mine the data on the chain in depth.

4.4.3 Data Storage

In this era of big data, a lot of data is generated by devices in the Internet of things. Most of these devices have limited storage resources, which are hard to store the whole ledger. Due to the limited computing and storage capacity, a lightweight and adaptive blockchain security solution is needed (Tariq et al., 2019). In the aspect of commercial application, the network nodes of blockchain need to store all blockchain information, which leads to a very limited number of parallel transactions. With the increase of blockchain size, the demand for storage, bandwidth and computing power of network nodes also increases. Therefore, it is necessary to design a blockchain service solution in the future, which uses distributed security authentication technology to achieve fragmentation and partial storage (Zhao & Meng, 2019). In some blockchain applications that track data changes, data version control is very important (S. Wang et al., 2018). Without version control, a large amount of redundant data may be generated, which wastes storage space. One of the main challenges to support data versioning is to reduce storage overhead. Only the improvement of storage technology can make these applications have a longer-term development.

4.4.4 Consensus Upgrade

A consensus algorithm can be defined as a mechanism to make multiple participants in the network reach an agreement. Since the public blockchain does not rely on a central authority, the decentralised nodes need to reach an agreement on the validity of the transaction. This is the role of the consensus algorithm to ensure that all nodes comply with the protocol rules and that all transactions are conducted in a reliable way. When blockchain technology is applied to the field of big data, there must be multiple participants in the network. How to make these participants reach an agreement on one problem is a big problem. In the blockchain world, the consensus mechanism is a solution to this problem. If the problem of consensus mechanism is not solved, the combination of blockchain and big data is meaningless. The most widely used consensus algorithms are POW and POS. Other consensus algorithms utilise the alternative implementation of POW and POS, as well as other hybrid implementations and some new consensus strategies (Bach et al., 2018), such as Ripple protocol consensus algorithm RPCA (Schwartz, Youngs, & Britto, 2014), Stellar Consensus Protocol (SCP) (Mazieres, 2015), Delegated Proof of Stake (DPOS) (Larimer, 2018), and so on. Each industry will select and modify the consensus mechanism according to its own needs. A Proof of Disease (PoD) consensus protocol (Talukder, Chaitanya, Arnold, & Sakurai, 2018) is a blockchain consensus protocol for accurate medical decisions and reducing the disease burden. It was created to solve the problem of information exchange in the medical field. Proof-of-Trust Consensus Protocol (Zou et al., 2018) is a blockchain consensus protocol for enhancing accountability in crowdsourcing services. It provides a viable accountability solution for the online service industry. Proof of Authentication (PoAh) consensus protocol (Puthal & Mohanty, 2018) is a blockchain consensus protocol for the lightweight implementation of blockchains in the Internet of Things. The proof-of-benefit consensus mechanism with an online benefit generating (ONPoB) algorithm (Liu et al., 2019) is an electric vehicle charging solution. It was created to handle the electric vehicle charging/discharging loads to flatten the overall power load fluctuation. However, participants and their big data environment are constantly changing, that is to say, there may be some changes in industry rules and their own adjustments. After all parties of the blockchain have reached a consensus, how to upgrade the consensus with the changes of environment is a very important issue. Especially after joining the incentive mechanism, how to persuade stakeholders to revise their opinions needs further research and discussion.

4.4.5 Intensified Competition

Data is undoubtedly the foundation of the information society. Each enterprise wants to collect as much data as possible to improve its competitiveness in the future (Lecuyer et al., 2018). With the dual support of the concepts of 'blockchain' and 'big data', increasingly start-ups enter the blockchain and big data arena. At present, the profit route of big data companies can be summarised as 'data-tools-services'. Data acquisition is the first barrier to competition. In many areas, whether the data can be obtained or not determines the survival of the enterprise, such as medical data, civil aviation data and other areas with high data acquisition barriers. However, in the blockchain industry, due to the characteristics of the technology itself, there is basically no threshold for big data companies to acquire data. That is, everyone can access the data on the blockchain. Breaking the data barrier means the reduction of data costs. In the future, increasingly blockchain big data enterprises will appear, and the competition among enterprises will be significantly fierce. How to deal with data is the focus of competition, that is to say, who can provide more accurate and valuable content and tools are the key to win blockchain big data. However, for blockchain big data service companies, it is still early days, and there are still many things to be done.

4.5 CHAPTER SUMMARY

Big data without a clear value attribute is just a bunch of data. In essence, there are some bottlenecks and challenges in the development of big data at the present stage, which are related to the fact that the value of big data itself (especially for different dimensions) cannot be well-reflected. The unclear interest relationship and the blocking of interest realisation channels make it difficult for the relevant subjects of big data to form a resultant force and break through the obstacles to promote the development of big data.

Due to its advantages in ownership determination, data security, and transaction flexibility, blockchain technology has obvious help for the display and realisation of data value. The combination of blockchain and big data can make a great contribution to the value interconnection of the future society.

This chapter introduced the business value of blockchain and introduced in-depth thinking with TCP/IP. If we look back at the development history and network composition of Internet technology and compare the current blockchain technology with the increasingly hot concept of value interconnection, we can find that blockchain technology is indeed likely to become the future TCP/IP of value Internet. Blockchain technology can make assets intelligent, connects the machine economy, and optimises the social structure. This chapter also discusses some of the changes that blockchain can bring to big data. For example, it can make data more secure and reliable, as well as facilitate data sharing and data analysis. Finally, we think blockchain technology can reshape the big data industry and give some of our ideas.

REFERENCES

Androulaki, E., Barger, A., Bortnikov, V., Cachin, C., Christidis, K., De Caro, A., . . . Manevich, Y. (2018). Hyperledger fabric: A distributed operating system for permissioned blockchains. *Paper presented at the Proceedings of the Thirteenth EuroSys Conference.*

Azaria, A., Ekblaw, A., Vieira, T., & Lippman, A. (2016). Medrec: Using blockchain for medical data access and permission management. *Paper presented at the 2016 2nd International Conference on Open and Big Data (OBD).*

Bach, L., Mihaljevic, B., & Zagar, M. (2018). Comparative analysis of blockchain consensus algorithms. *Paper presented at the 2018 41st International Convention on Information and Communication Technology, Electronics and Microelectronics (MIPRO).*

Bandara, E., Ng, W. K., De Zoysa, K., Fernando, N., Tharaka, S., Maurakirinathan, P., & Jayasuriya, N. (2018). Mystiko—Blockchain meets big data. *Paper presented at the 2018 IEEE International Conference on Big Data (Big Data).*

Chen, Y., Ding, S., Xu, Z., Zheng, H., & Yang, S. (2019). Blockchain-based medical records secure storage and medical service framework. *Journal of Medical Systems, 43*(1), 5.

Cichosz, S. L., Stausholm, M. N., Kronborg, T., Vestergaard, P., & Hejlesen, O. (2019). How to use blockchain for diabetes health care data and access management: An operational concept. *Journal of Diabetes Science and Technology, 13*(2), 248–253.

Dagher, G. G., Mohler, J., Milojkovic, M., & Marella, P. B. (2018). Ancile: Privacy-preserving framework for access control and interoperability of electronic health records using blockchain technology. *Sustainable Cities and Society, 39,* 283–297.

Fedak, V. (2018). Blockchain and big data: The match made in heavens. Towards Data Science. https://towardsdatascience.com/blockchain-and-big-data-the-match-made-in-heavens-337887a0ce73.

Grishin, D., Obbad, K., Estep, P., Quinn, K., Zaranek, S. W., Zaranek, A. W., . . . Cifric, M. (2018). Accelerating genomic data generation and facilitating genomic data access using decentralization, privacy-preserving technologies and equitable compensation. *Blockchain in Healthcare Today. 1*, 1–23.

Hassani, H., Huang, X., & Silva, E. (2018). Banking with blockchain-ed big data. *Journal of Management Analytics, 5*(4), 256–275.

Huang, Z. (2019). From Data Science to Blockchain–Analytics in Cross-Border Logistics [w:]. In *Proceedings of the 8th SIGKDD International Workshop on Urban Computing (UrbComp'19)*. http://urban.cs.wpi.edu/urbcomp2019/.

Iansiti, M., & Lakhani, K. R. (2017). The truth about blockchain. *Harvard Business Review, 95*(1), 118–127.

Khan, R., & Mittelman, D. (2018). Consumer genomics will change your life, whether you get tested or not. *Genome Biology, 19*(1), 120.

Larimer, D. (2018). DPOS Consensus Algorithm—The Missing Whitepaper. Steemit (2018).

Lecuyer, M., Spahn, R., Geambasu, R., Huang, T.-K., & Sen, S. (2018). Enhancing selectivity in big data. *IEEE Security & Privacy, 16*(1), 34–42.

Liu, C., Chai, K. K., Zhang, X., & Chen, Y. (2019). Proof-of-benefit: A blockchain-enabled EV charging scheme. *Paper presented at the 2019 IEEE 89th Vehicular Technology Conference (VTC2019-Spring)*.

Maesa, D. D. F., Mori, P., & Ricci, L. (2019). A blockchain based approach for the definition of auditable Access Control systems. *Computers & Security, 84*, 93–119.

Mazieres, D. (2015). The stellar consensus protocol: A federated model for internet-level consensus. *Stellar Development Foundation, 32*, 1–32.

McConaghy, T., Marques, R., Müller, A., De Jonghe, D., McConaghy, T., McMullen, G., . . . Granzotto, A. (2016). BigchainDB: a scalable blockchain database. White paper, BigChainDB.

Mengelkamp, E., Notheisen, B., Beer, C., Dauer, D., & Weinhardt, C. (2018). A blockchain-based smart grid: towards sustainable local energy markets. *Computer Science-Research and Development, 33*(1–2), 207–214.

Moreno, J., Serrano, M. A., Fernandez, E. B., & Fernández-Medina, E. (2020). Improving incident response in big data ecosystems by using blockchain technologies. *Applied Sciences, 10*(2), 724.

Puthal, D., & Mohanty, S. P. (2018). Proof of authentication: IoT-friendly blockchains. *IEEE Potentials, 38*(1), 26–29.

Raghupathi, W., & Raghupathi, V. (2014). Big data analytics in healthcare: Promise and potential. *Health Information Science and Systems, 2*(1), 3.

Sahoo, M. S., & Baruah, P. K. (2018). HBasechainDB–A scalable blockchain framework on Hadoop ecosystem. *Paper presented at the Asian Conference on Supercomputing Frontiers*.

Sawa, T. (2019). Blockchain technology outline and its application to field of power and energy system. *Electrical Engineering in Japan, 206*(2), 11–15.

Schwartz, D., Youngs, N., & Britto, A. (2014). The ripple protocol consensus algorithm. *Ripple Labs Inc White Paper, 5*, 8.

Talukder, A. K., Chaitanya, M., Arnold, D., & Sakurai, K. (2018). Proof of disease: A blockchain consensus protocol for accurate medical decisions and reducing the disease burden. *Paper presented at the 2018 IEEE SmartWorld, Ubiquitous Intelligence & Computing, Advanced & Trusted Computing, Scalable Computing & Communications, Cloud & Big Data Computing, Internet of People and Smart City Innovation (SmartWorld/SCALCOM/UI C/ATC/CBDCom/IOP/SCI).*

Tapscott, A., & Tapscott, D. (2017). How blockchain is changing finance. *Harvard Business Review, 1*(9), 2–5.

Tariq, N., Asim, M., Al-Obeidat, F., Zubair Farooqi, M., Baker, T., Hammoudeh, M., & Ghafir, I. (2019). The security of big data in fog-enabled IoT applications including blockchain: A survey. *Sensors, 19*(8), 1788.

Uchibeke, U. U., Schneider, K. A., Kassani, S. H., & Deters, R. (2018). Blockchain access control ecosystem for big data security. *Paper presented at the 2018 IEEE International Conference on Internet of Things (iThings) and IEEE Green Computing and Communications (GreenCom) and IEEE Cyber, Physical and Social Computing (CPSCom) and IEEE Smart Data (SmartData).*

Wang, S., Dinh, T. T. A., Lin, Q., Xie, Z., Zhang, M., Cai, Q., . . . Ruan, P. (2018). Forkbase: An efficient storage engine for blockchain and forkable applications. *Proceedings of the VLDB Endowment, 11*(10), 1137–1150.

Wang, X., Hu, Q., Zhang, Y., Zhang, G., Juan, W., & Xing, C. (2018). A kind of decision model research based on big data and blockchain in eHealth. *Paper presented at the International Conference on Web Information Systems and Applications.*

Xia, Q., Sifah, E. B., Asamoah, K. O., Gao, J., Du, X., & Guizani, M. (2017). MeDShare: Trust-less medical data sharing among cloud service providers via blockchain. *IEEE Access, 5*, 14757–14767.

Zamani, M., Movahedi, M., & Raykova, M. (2018). Rapidchain: Scaling blockchain via full sharding. *Paper presented at the Proceedings of the 2018 ACM SIGSAC Conference on Computer and Communications Security.*

Zhang, A., & Lin, X. (2018). Towards secure and privacy-preserving data sharing in e-health systems via consortium blockchain. *Journal of Medical Systems, 42*(8), 140.

Zhao, C., & Meng, X. (2019). Research on innovation and development of blockchain technology in financial field. *Paper presented at the 2019 International Conference on Pedagogy, Communication and Sociology (ICPCS 2019).*

Zou, J., Ye, B., Qu, L., Wang, Y., Orgun, M. A., & Li, L. (2018). A proof-of-trust consensus protocol for enhancing accountability in crowdsourcing services. *IEEE Transactions on Services Computing, 12*(3), 429–445.

CHAPTER 5

Applications of Blockchain Technology

B LOCKCHAIN SYSTEM IS FEATURED by distributed high redundancy storage, time-series data, non-tampering and forgery, and decentralisation and privacy protection, which makes blockchain technology not only successfully applied in the field of digital cryptocurrency but also widely applied in economic, financial, and social systems. The following chapter will introduce changes in the financial industry, Internet of Things, smart healthcare, supply chain, management, and trading of digital assets.

5.1 CHANGES IN THE FINANCIAL INDUSTRY

The essence of finance is business credit. Under most scenarios, the establishment of transaction credit basically depends on third-party intermediary institutions including financial institutions. The main pain points facing the financial sector at the present stage are as follows: first, it is difficult to verify the authenticity of assets and transaction information, which leads to high cost of credit assessment and the difficulty of implementing inclusive financial services. Second, the business process of cross-institutional financial transactions is complex and the cycle is long, resulting in low efficiency. Third, the cross-border operation and development of Internet finance have brought challenges to the traditional centralised risk management and supervision model.

The emergence of blockchain makes it possible for fusion innovation in many scenarios that are difficult to be integrated online due to trust granularity or trust cost in the traditional Internet. For the realised financial scenario, blockchain provides a scheme to transfer the 'foundation of trust' from high offline cost to low online costs. While reducing credit cost, the multi-party sharing feature of blockchain also strengthens the connection and collaboration between participants and improves the efficiency of value exchange. At the same time, blockchain provides a foundation for innovation in a wide range of business scenarios in the financial field that rely on trust and also makes it possible to innovate business models that integrate across industries in the future.

The application of blockchain in the financial field covers the business directions of supply chain finance, trade finance, digital bills, payment and settlement, digital assets, credit investigation and management, and so on.

5.1.1 Supply Chain Finance

Supply chain finance refers to the comprehensive financial products and services provided to the upstream and downstream enterprises of the supply chain by taking the core enterprises and their related upstream and downstream enterprises as a whole, relying on the core enterprises and taking real trade as the premise, and using self-compensating trade financing.

Blockchain technology is used to realise credit penetration upstream and downstream of the supply chain and solve the financing difficulties and high financing costs for upstream multi-level suppliers. The blockchain-based solution is mainly composed of data and business, and the related process is shown in Figure 5.1.

In terms of data, data from the four streams of the supply chain in the business process (information flow, commercial flow, logistics, and capital flow) and financing data will be up-linked, taking advantage of the difficult tampering and distributed nature of blockchain to improve data credibility and solve the pain point of information fragmentation.

In terms of business, the hard-to-tamper-tamper traceability of blockchain converts core enterprise credit (bills, credit lines or confirmations of payables) into digital certificates, enabling credit to be effectively transmitted along the supply chain, reducing cooperation costs and realising credit connectivity.

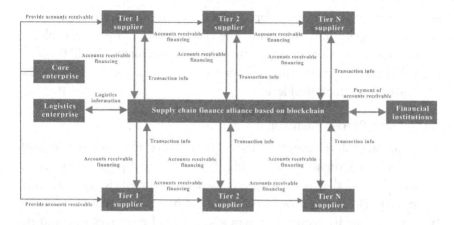

FIGURE 5.1 The blockchain-based solution and the related process.

To a certain extent, the new type of supply chain finance on blockchain realises the mechanism of accurate transmission of business information of real industries to financial institutions, which helps to solve the financing difficulties of small and micro enterprises, promotes better financial services for the real economy, effectively prevents the counterfeiting of bills and contracts, expands the business sources, customer channels and business scale of financial institutions, and realises a win-win situation for small and micro enterprises, core enterprises and financial institutions.

5.1.2 Digital Bill

The bill is an important financial product in the financial market, which has the dual function of payment and financing and has the characteristics of high value, bank credit, or commercial credit. Once an instrument is issued, its face value, date and other important information cannot be changed. Once the transaction is completed, the transaction cannot be revoked. There are two characteristics of the notes in circulation: first, the circulation of the notes mainly occurs in bank acceptances, and the number and circulation of commercial acceptances are relatively small; second, the credit and risk control of the note business is carried out independently by each bank, and the results of the wind control of a single bank may affect other participants in the transaction chain of the note market.

The characteristics of the instrument dictate that its face information and transaction information must be complete and unalterable. Compared to normal financial transactions, the amount of money transacted in bills is generally larger and therefore security requirements are higher. The security, integrity, and non-tampering characteristics provided by blockchain through cryptography can meet these requirements for bill transactions to a certain extent, thus helping to prevent and control risks in the bill business at a technical level.

5.1.3 Cross-Border Payment

With the rapid development of cross-border trade activities, the scale of cross-border payments is expanding, and traditional payment products are facing the challenges of long processes and slow efficiency, especially when the bookkeeping process is carried out by both sides of the transaction, which usually requires human and material resources to complete the reconciliation across multiple institutions due to information asymmetry, and is prone to inconsistent reconciliation, which affects settlement efficiency.

The cross-agency payment clearing platform based on blockchain technology can directly share transaction data flow between the two parties, simplify the reconciliation process, and serve as an effective supplement to traditional payment products.

Some financial institutions have actively explored the application of blockchain technology to the reconciliation of accounts among financial institutions and cross-border remittance services and achieved good results.

In addition, the company has developed a blockchain cross-border wallet project for China Merchants Bank, a blockchain platform for China Merchants Bank's Direct Union Pay blockchain, a reconciliation platform between financial institutions for WeBank and a blockchain cross-border remittance service platform for China UnionPay for Hyperchain Technology.

5.2 INTERNET OF THINGS

The Internet of Things (IoT) has encountered the following five industry pain points during its long-term evolution: device security, personal privacy, architectural rigidity, communication compatibility and multi-entity collaboration.

In terms of device security, the Mirai-created Botnets of Things, named by MIT Technology Review as one of the top ten breakthrough technologies of 2017, has cumulatively infected more than 2 million cameras and other IoT devices, according to statistics, with a DDoS attack launched by the Mirai botnet that crippled US domain resolution service provider Dyn. Twitter, Paypal, and several other popular websites were inaccessible at the time. This was followed by botnets that enslaved IoT devices and allowed them to mine Bitcoin, and the larger and more active http81 botnet, among others.

In terms of personal privacy, mainly because the centralised management structure is unable to prove itself, there have been relevant times when personal data has been compromised. In the recent past, the Chinese People's Daily reported that 266 cameras in Chengdu were webcast live is a case in point.

In terms of architectural rigidity, current IoT data streams are aggregated to a single central control system, and with the continued evolution of low-power wide-area technology (LPWA), it is foreseeable that future IoT devices will grow geometrically and the cost of centralised services will be unaffordable. IBM predicts that there will be more than 25 billion devices connected to the Internet of Everything in 2020.

In terms of communication compatibility, the lack of a unified language for global IoT platforms can easily result in multiple IoT devices being blocked from communicating with each other and creating multiple competing standards and platforms.

In terms of multi-entity collaboration, much of the IoT is currently a self-organising network within operators and enterprises. When it comes to collaboration across multiple operators and between multiple peers, the cost of establishing credit is high.

Blockchain, by virtue of its characteristics of subject peering, openness and transparency, secure communication, difficult tampering and multi-party consensus, will have an important impact on the IoT: the qualities of multi-centricity and weak centralisation will reduce the high operation and maintenance costs of centralised architectures, the qualities of information encryption and secure communication will help protect privacy, and identity rights management and multi-party consensus will help identify illegal nodes and promptly block access and mischief from malicious nodes. The structure of relying on chains helps to build traceable electronic evidence storage, and the distributed architecture and subject peer-to-peer features help to break the shackles of multiple information silos existing in the Internet of Things, promoting horizontal information flow and multi-party collaboration.

5.2.1 Documentation and Traceability of Sensor Data

Traditional supply chain transportation needs to go through multiple entities, such as shippers, carriers, freight forwarders, shipping agents, yards, shipping companies, land transportation (collection card) companies, and banks that do business roles such as manifest mortgage financing. Many of the information systems between these subjects are independent of each other and are not interconnected. On the one hand, there is the problem of data forgery, on the other hand, because of the lack of data interoperability, emergency response cannot respond in a timely manner when the situation arises. In this application scenario, deploying blockchain nodes to each subject in the supply chain, through real-time (e.g., when the ship docks) and offline (e.g., when the ship is operating in the distant sea), and so on, the data collected by the sensors will be written into the blockchain and become electronic evidence that cannot be tampered with, which can enhance the cost of counterfeiting and denial by all parties and further clarify the boundaries of responsibility of all parties, while at the same time enabling the structure of the blockchain to be adopted. Traceability, keeping abreast of the latest developments in logistics, taking the necessary response measures based on the data collected in real-time (e.g., in cold chain transport, cargo holds above 0°C are immediately checked for the source of the malfunction), and enhancing the potential for multi-party collaboration.

5.2.2 Smart Meter-Based Energy Trading

Primarily, the traditional transmission has a line loss rate of 5%, and surplus energy from microgrids built by households cannot be stored or shared with other households with energy needs. A partnership between New York startup LO3 Energy and ConsenSys, with LO3 Energy taking care of energy-related controls and ConsenSys providing the underlying blockchain technology, has enabled a peer-to-peer transaction, automated execution, and energy trading platform without third-party intermediaries in Brooklyn, New York, enabling energy transactions and sharing among ten households. The main implementation is to install smart meters at the door of each household, and the smart meters install blockchain software to form a blockchain network. The user issues the corresponding smart contract on the blockchain node of his own smart meter through the mobile phone app, and based on the contract rules, the corresponding link connection is controlled through the grid equipment provided by Siemens to realise energy trading and energy supply.

5.2.3 Safe Communication and Group Intelligence for Drones

Machine-to-machine communication must be considered from two perspectives: on the one hand, every drone has a built-in hardware key. The identity ID derived from the private key enhances identity authentication, and digital signature-based communication ensures secure interaction and prevents the proliferation of forged information and access to illegal devices. On the other hand, based on the consensus mechanism of the blockchain, the future of blockchain and artificial intelligence is the point of combination – group intelligence.

But, blockchain with IoT will encounter the following four challenges.

In terms of resource consumption, IoT devices generally suffer from low computing power, weak networking capabilities, and short battery life. Bitcoin's Proof of Workload (PoW) mechanism is too large for resource consumption and is obviously otherwise applicable to deployment in IoT nodes and possibly in servers such as IoT gateways. Secondly, blockchain 2.0 technologies such as ethereum are also PoW+PoS and are gradually switching to PoS. Distributed architectures require consensus mechanisms to ensure the ultimate consistency of data, however, the consumption of resources is not negligible relative to centralised architectures.

In terms of data storage, blockchain is a data storage technology that can only be attached and not deleted. As the blockchain continues to grow, IoT devices may not have enough storage space. For example, Bitcoin runs to date and requires more than 300 GB of physical storage space.

In terms of performance bottlenecks, the traditional bitcoin transaction is seven transactions per second, plus consensus confirmation, it takes about 1 hour to write to the blockchain, this kind of delay caused by feedback delay, alarm delay, in the delay-sensitive industrial Internet is not feasible.

In terms of partition tolerance, industrial IoT emphasises that the nodes are always online, but it is common for ordinary IoT nodes to fail and frequently join and leave the network, which is prone to network turbulence that consumes a large amount of network bandwidth and even network fragmentation.

5.3 SMART HEALTHCARE

With the development of the Internet, the degree of digitisation in the healthcare field has increased, and the trend of electronification is becoming more and more obvious, both from the point of view of medical equipment and medical services. However, due to the low degree of digitisation, there is an obvious asymmetry of information among hospitals. This brings a huge waste of human and material resources, reduces the efficiency of the industry, and hinders the rapid development of the industry.

The blockchain can protect patient privacy using features such as anonymity and decentralisation, and solve the current shortcomings of smart medical care. For the healthcare industry, blockchain has three very important advantages.

First, the data on the blockchain cannot be tampered with. While we rarely hear about real-world incidents of medical data falsification and medical record tampering, there's no avoiding the fact that these grey areas do exist. Medical data has the potential to be tampered with and compromised whenever human-to-human operations are involved, and it's clear that either one can cause harm to patients. The fact that the blockchain cannot be tampered with, cannot be undone, and every action is recorded, allows the accuracy and uniqueness of medical data to be guaranteed.

Second, high redundancy. Because every node in the blockchain is backed up, this makes it so that a single point of failure does not compromise the integrity of the data, which ensures that the data of that user is not lost, as the loss of a single independent node does not result in the loss of the blockchain as a whole. The private key in the hands of that user, on the other hand, ensures the security of the blockchain as a whole in which only the private key holder is entitled to view the data.

Third, the complex permissions of multiple private key holders. Imagine a very dangerous state of affairs in today's Internet society, where all sensitive health-related data such as identity characteristics, disease conditions, treatment options, payment status and health insurance can be accessed and used effortlessly, and the blockchain multi-private key authority custody model can put an end to this very scenario.

With a single smart contract, it is possible to assign multiple private keys to a single piece of informational data and set up a rule that every time access is made to that data, you must be authorised by your private key to do so.

Electronic health records (EHRs), drug traceability, and DNA wallets are all possible application areas for blockchain technology.

5.3.1 EHR

Electronic health cases are the most important application of blockchain in healthcare.

In traditional healthcare, a patient's medical information is in the hands of the hospital where he or she is being treated, and since prescriptions and cases are fundamental to the hospital, as well as the privacy of medical information and legal constraints, these factors make it difficult for hospitals to disclose medical information easily. Therefore, there has always been a problem of poor flow of medical information and information leakage.

In terms of EHR, an individual's complete health history is of great value for precise treatment and disease prevention, and blockchain can do the job of storing and sharing this data in real-time.

Each event in the blockchain is time-stamped, generating a long chain through the extension of the block, which cannot be tampered with, and if it is a public chain, no permissions are required and all computers can access to view the records, and if it is a union chain, permissions can be set to maintain privacy. In short, the blockchain can achieve the whole process of medical information records, including the patient's medical records and medical supplies throughout the supply chain process.

1. The blockchain's immutability ensures the authenticity and integrity of medical information.

2. Blockchain can be encrypted with multiple private keys, and user private key authorisation is required to view the user's data on the chain, which can ensure the legal circulation and use of the user's sensitive data, and will not be leaked to criminals or used maliciously, because if enterprises or organisations need to view the user's medical information, these actions will be recorded on the blockchain, and can be traced back to the source in case of problems.

5.3.2 Drug Anti-Counterfeit Traceability

For example, the establishment of a drug consistency logistics and distribution and management system constitutes a fatal blow to counterfeit drugs. Because blockchain data is instantly updated and widely shared, pharmacies, manufacturers, buyers, regulators and other parties can observe the flow of data in real-time, including drug manufacturing and distribution information, thereby strengthening drug regulation and preventing counterfeit drugs from entering the market. Blockverify in the UK is said to be one of the organisations conducting a pilot program to source medicines, helping healthcare professionals verify the authenticity of drugs by scanning them.

5.3.3 DNA Wallet

Genetic and medical data can be securely stored using blockchain technology and accessed through the use of private secret keys, which will create a DNA wallet. This allows healthcare providers to securely share and count patient data, helping drug companies to develop drugs more efficiently, and this model is gradually being established.

5.4 SUPPLY CHAIN

The supply chain is a functional network structure that connects suppliers, manufacturers, distributors and end-users into an integrated whole from matching parts, intermediate products to final products around the core enterprise, and finally from the sales network to the consumers. This is illustrated in Figure 5.2.

Supply chains, which link complex actors (both individuals and businesses) to supply, manufacture, distribution, retail and customers, are bound to vary greatly from product to product, and may span hundreds of stages for complex products, with a cycle lasting several months or more and involving multiple geographic locations around the world.

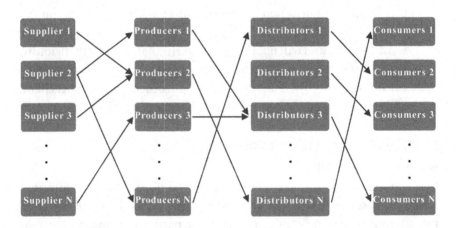

FIGURE 5.2   Relationship in supply chain.

Throughout the process, the basic components of the supply chain are logistics, information flow, and capital flow. Logistics flows from upstream suppliers to downstream retailers until it reaches the final customer, capital flows from downstream to upstream, and information flows in both directions. In the supply chain, information flow, logistics and capital flow are the three main lifelines, information flow to direct logistics, logistics to drive capital flow.

1. Information flow: In the circulation of goods, the flow of all information is referred to as information flow. It includes the supply and demand information and management information in the supply chain, which is produced continuously along with the operation of logistics, throughout the whole process of commodity trading, recording the flow of the whole business activities, and is an important basis for analyzing logistics, guiding capital flow and making business decisions.

2. Logistics: It is the goods from the supply to the receiving entity flow process, according to the actual needs, the transportation, storage, handling, packaging, circulation, processing, distribution, information processing and other functions organically combined to achieve the user requirements of the process. Modern logistics is a product of economic globalisation and an important service industry that promotes economic globalisation.

3. Flow of funds: the process of monetary circulation, funds are the blood of the enterprise, the flow of funds is the key to revitalise a supply chain. The operation status of the enterprise's money flow in the supply chain is directly influenced by its upstream chain and downstream chain, and the efficiency and dynamic optimisation degree of the upstream chain and downstream chain's money operation are directly related to the operation quality of the enterprise's money flow.

The supply chain consists of many participating subjects, and there are a large number of exchanges and cooperation between different subjects. In practice, supply chain information flow blockage is not smooth, logistics inefficiency, and capital flow problems occur from time to time.

Blockchain technology naturally meets the needs of supply chain management. First of all, the chain structure of blockchain can be understood as a kind of time-series data that can store information. This has similarities to the form of product flow in a supply chain. Secondly, the relatively low frequency of information updates in the supply chain avoids the shortcomings of current blockchain technology in terms of processing performance. From an enterprise's perspective, knowing the status of goods in real-time can help enterprises optimise production operations and management and improve efficiency. Promoting blockchain technology is in the interests of all business entities.

Information about every transaction on the blockchain (parties, time of the transaction, the content of the transaction, etc.) is recorded on a block and stored on a distributed ledger at each node in the chain, which ensures integrity, reliability, and high transparency of the information. These features of blockchain make its application among the supply chain has many advantages.

1. Information sharing, help improve system efficiency: blockchain is a kind of distributed ledger, that is, the information on the blockchain (ledger) by the various participants at the same time recording, sharing. The use of blockchain technology in supply chain management enables information to be made public between upstream and downstream enterprises. As a result, information such as demand changes can be reflected to each entity in the chain in real-time, and each enterprise can keep abreast of the latest progress in logistics in order to take appropriate measures. Similar to the VMI (Vendor Managed Inventory) strategy, this approach enhances the potential for multi-party collaboration, information visualisation, process optimisation and demand management, and improves the overall efficiency of the system.

2. Multi-principal participation in monitoring and auditing, effectively prevent transaction injustice, transaction fraud and other problems: in traditional transactions, a single central body is usually used to achieve the authentication of trading behaviour. The certification centre requires higher operation and maintenance costs, has limited access to data, and has the possibility of data being tampered with, stolen, or destroyed by criminals, which is an obstacle for enterprises to share data (Figure 5.3).

Compared with the traditional independent centre certification, blockchain-based supply chain multi-centre collaborative certification

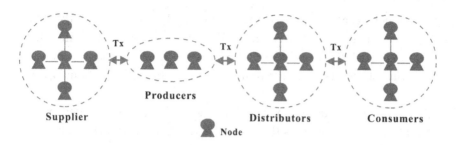

FIGURE 5.3   Network node relationship in supply chain.

system does not need to entrust a third party as an independent certification centre, by the parties to the transaction as different certification centre to certify the supply chain transaction behaviour. Upstream and downstream enterprises of the supply chain to establish an alliance chain, only within the supply chain business entities to participate in the alliance chain to jointly confirm the members of the management, certification, authorisation and other actions. By putting materials, logistics, transactions and other information records on the chain, the information upstream and downstream of the supply chain is open among enterprises, so that the monitoring, auditing and other functions can be jointly notarised by the subjects of the transaction. In this way, the competition between the various nodes to keep accounts, power equality, the certification body composed of multiple trading subjects can effectively prevent unfair transactions, transaction fraud and other issues. If a trading entity alone or jointly with other trading entities attempts to tamper with transaction records, other trading entities can prove their wrongdoing based on their own records of transactions and clean up the supply chain.

3. To ensure the authenticity of data, to help solve product traceability, trading disputes and other issues: through the application of blockchain technology, the supply chain upstream and downstream information can be written in blocks (such as March 25 in a certain year, the supply chain on the transaction information written in a block, March 26, the transaction information written in the next block), and between the blocks and blocks by the chain connection. The content of the block and the chain information between the blocks are encrypted by means of Hash algorithm, and so on, which ensures that the content of the block cannot be deleted and the connection between the blocks is safe and reliable. As a result of the distributed

structure, all the participants in the supply chain have all the information stored in the chain, which further ensures the authenticity and reliability of the data. The above technology ensures that it is almost impossible to manipulate or destroy data for personal gain.

Therefore, in the supply chain, when the information provided by the Internet of Things, such as the source of goods, basic information, packing list information, transportation status and other information is accurate and reliable, the information will be uploaded and recorded in the blockchain, and blockchain technology can ensure that the subsequent dissemination of information, additions, and so on are secure and transparent. By reading the data on the chain, it can directly locate problems in the middle of the transportation process and avoid problems such as loss of goods, mis-claims, or commercial frauds. This technology is particularly applicable to the field of scarce goods, and by uploading data on production, logistics and sales, it can ensure the uniqueness of products, protect the rights and interests of consumers, and eliminate the possibility of circulation of counterfeit goods. In addition, when a transaction dispute occurs, it can be quickly forensic according to the information on the chain, clarify the responsibility of the main body, and improve the efficiency of payment, settlement, claims processing (Figure 5.4).

4. Reducing communication costs: On the one hand, blockchain technology can help upstream and downstream enterprises to establish a secure distributed ledger, and the information on the ledger is open to all parties to the transaction; on the other hand, through the smart contract technology, we can record the content of the agreement

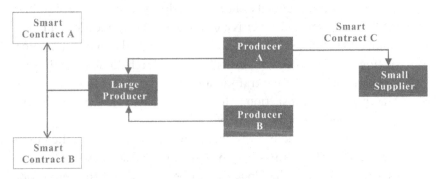

FIGURE 5.4   Smart contract relationship in supply chain.

between enterprises in the form of code on the ledger, once the conditions of the agreement, the information on the ledger takes effect and the code is executed automatically. For example, when a buyer makes a transaction from a supplier, a contract can be created on the chain, the content of which is that when logistics data indicates that the goods have arrived at the location, the payment is sent to the supplier. This way, as soon as the logistics arrival information is sent, the payment will be automatically transferred out. As the blockchain data is secure and immutable, the enforceability of the code on the smart contract makes it impossible to renege and break the contract. The use of smart contracts can be efficient real-time updates and less human intervention characteristics, enterprises can achieve the dynamic management of the supplier team, as well as the improvement of supply chain efficiency. The use of blockchain technology to register and share information about equipment and other related information of spare parts suppliers can help small enterprises with processing needs in the off-season to find suitable manufacturers directly, and even use smart contracts to automatically place orders for procurement, thereby achieving the purpose of accurate implementation of production plans. These small enterprises can skip the middlemen, thus saving costs; at the same time, this also helps activate the manufacturer's vacant capacity.

5.5 MANAGEMENT AND TRADING OF DIGITAL ASSETS

A digital asset is an economic resource that is owned or controlled by an enterprise or individual, exists as electronic data, and is measured in money. Both digital and physical assets suffer from poor asset liquidity and financing problems that arise either from the physical existence of the asset or from the way it is issued and circulated.

Traditional asset services such as proof of ownership and proof of authenticity require the intervention of relevant intermediaries to complete. The existence of a large number of centralised credit and information intermediaries reduces the efficiency of information transmission and increases the cost of asset services. The circulation of assets requires the intervention of at least the issuer, the recipient, and the flow of assets.

It can only be completed with the participation of the three parties involved in the circulation platform, because of the lack of open and transparent information in the circulation process, resulting in the inability of the participants to accurately grasp the historical information and real-time performance of assets, hindering the pricing and rating process of assets, resulting in a lack of investment confidence in the market and reducing the liquidity of assets.

Using blockchain technology to build a decentralised digital asset network, allowing multiple parties, including asset issuers, asset traders, exchanges, and distribution channels, to participate and conduct business on the chain according to their roles, realising the registration, issuance, circulation, and settlement of digital assets. Through the blockchain digital asset network, banks, enterprises and even individuals can issue digital assets; taking advantage of blockchain's multi-party sharing and difficult to tamper with features, asset registration is publicised, and the transfer and settlement of digital assets is completed on the blockchain network in the form of transactions, effectively reducing asset disputes, ensuring the safety of digital assets and improving the efficiency of digital asset transfer. It provides more possibilities for adding value to digital assets and creating richer financial products and services. The traceable nature of blockchain transactions provides asset regulators with clear data details of the transaction links, strengthening the audit function and efficiency of asset regulators.

There are many problems in the field of digital asset trading, such as difficulties in copyright registration and protection, lack of integrity awareness of network transactions, small and micro works are difficult to be managed and authorised, infringement proof is difficult and the cost of defending rights and so on. The blockchain has a unique decentralised technical features, making each node work alone, nodes do not have superior and inferior links between nodes, a single node failure, the other nodes can still work normally, to ensure the safety of its processing and storage data. Its decentralised technology application, equal oversight of data and the protection of data security make it a natural advantage in enhancing the efficiency of data flow and digital security. Therefore, the introduction of blockchain into digital asset transactions has a certain degree of feasibility and necessity.

5.6 APPLICATION IN SMART CITY ROADSIDE PARKING

As society grows, the number of cars continues to increase. And this has also increased congestion in the city, making parking car more of a problem. There are two main types of city parking: parking lots and roadside parking. The parking lots have gradually realised intelligent management and improved operational efficiency through gates and scanning code payment methods. However, for urban roadside parking, manual charging is still the mainstay. This type obviously suffers from inefficiencies, opaque transactions, and so on.

Because Blockchain is distributed, unalterable, secure and trustworthy, it can provide reliability assurance for parking data. Based on this, it is a very good way to use blockchain technology to realise the roadside parking management system.

Di Yang et al. (Yang et al. 2020) designed and implemented a roadside parking management system based on Hyperledger Fabric consortium chain. They fully analysed the characteristics of roadside parking scenes and the current situation of Fabric, proposed such scheme.

The system is oriented to the roadside parking management application scene, after registering and binding the vehicle information through the client, the user will park in the roadside parking space. The parking information is captured by the edge camera, recognised by the edge server's license plate recognition algorithm, and sent to the webserver. The web server stores the parking transaction information and stores the hash digest to the blockchain. In summary, the architecture of the system design is shown in Figure 5.5.

The system uses a web server as the architecture backbone and receives parking transaction information from edge servers via Nginx gateway. Each edge server is connected to a number of camera networks to collect dynamic parking information metadata captured by the cameras. The metadata is periodically saved for review through the built-in storage space, and the license plate recognition algorithm is integrated to enable license plate number recognition at the edge-end. The recognised license plate number and other parking transaction information are uploaded to the web server and stored in MySQL database. The web server interacts with the Fabric consortium chain via a middleware SDK to achieve hash digest storage on blockchain. In addition, the webserver also receives service access requests from the client and the management-end and returns relevant results according to the request to realise the front-end presentation of the service.

The system mainly consists of four modules: edge-end, Fabric blockchain, web server and the client, as shown in Figure 5.6.

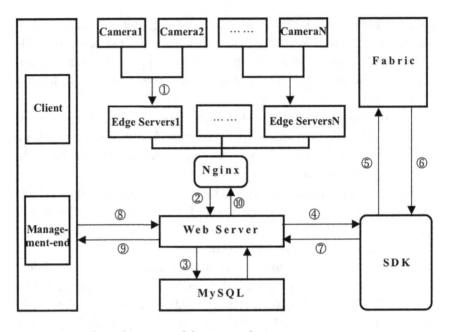

FIGURE 5.5   The architecture of the system design.

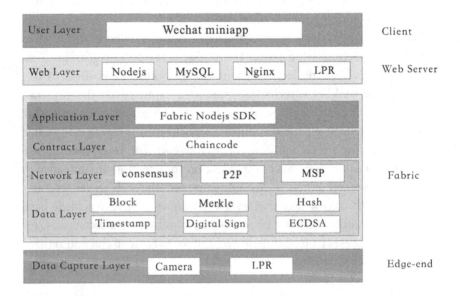

FIGURE 5.6   The module of the system.

5.6.1 Edge-End Module

The edge-end module is the data collection layer of the system. Each edge server is networked with N cameras to form an edge node, which is connected to the web server via the Nginx service. The cameras capture parking information and send the video metadata to the connected edge servers. After receiving the data, the edge server uses a deep learning algorithm deployed on the edge server to identify the license plate number. The architecture is shown in the following Figure 5.7.

When the user parks the car, the camera recognises the license plate number and sends it to the web server; when the user finishes parking and drives away, the timestamp information will be sent to the web server again.

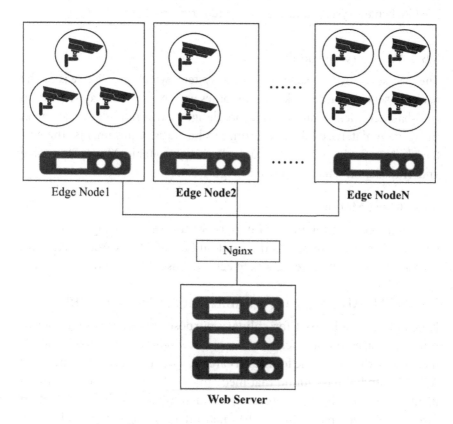

FIGURE 5.7   The architecture of the edge-end.

5.6.2 Fabric Module

This includes the data, network, contract, and application layers, whose function is to store data digest of the key parking data for verification. The data layer is the core part of the blockchain, which is used to store hash fingerprint information of transaction data. The network layer is the basis for information transmission on the Fabric blockchain platform, including the consensus mechanism, P2P network and the data validation mechanism in the network to achieve synchronisation and validation of block data between different nodes. The contract layer encapsulates a smart contract that enables system functionality, which is a piece of code that can perform operations such as validation, storage, and execution on the Fabric blockchain, and can interact with the Fabric network. The outermost layer is the Fabric SDK module, which is the connector between the blockchain system and the back-end services.

5.6.3 Web Server Module

The web server is the backbone of the system, which uses Node.js as the backend service framework and combines with Nginx gateway services to load-balance client requests. The core design of this module is mainly on the MySQL database table, according to business requirements, the system designs the User table, Cartable, ParkingInfo table, MoneyFlow table and Transaction table, as shown in Figure 5.8.

5.6.4 Client Module

The client provides interactive interface for users and managers. The system uses WeChat miniapp as the front-end framework, through API and Web server back-end interaction, to achieve business function.

5.7 APPLICATION IN TRACEABILITY OF CHINESE HERBS

Herbs are not only used for culinary purposes but are also an ancient source of spices and medicines. As socio-economic and ideological levels increase, herbal medicine for health care is gradually accepted. Numerous scientific studies have found that medicinal herbs and some of the ingredients they contain have preventive and inhibitory effects on certain diseases. Studies have shown that natural phenolic compounds from herbal medicine play an important role in cancer prevention and treatment (Huang, Cai, & Zhang, 2009; Tan et al. 2011). Some herbs such as

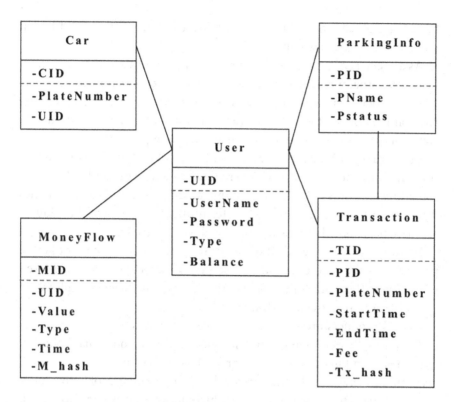

FIGURE 5.8 The design for database table.

Scutellaria baicalensis Georgi and its identified components which have been shown to inhibit the infectivity and replication of HIV (Wu, Attele, Zhang, & Yuan, 2001). In some Asian and African countries, medicinal herbs in Lamiaceae family have is commonly used to treat hypertension (Niazi, Yari, & Shakarami, 2019). Many reports have shown the positive effects of herbal extracts as an antiviral agent in animal feed or for prevention and treatment. The use of herbs may also reduce the development of drug resistance and may modulate the immune system to prevent virus-related diseases.

During the COVID-19 outbreak in early 2020, herbal medicine played an important role in the antiviral process. Of the more than 80,000 cases diagnosed in China, more than 70,000 were treated with herbal medicine, accounting for 91% of the total. More than 90% of patients in Hubei Province have received herbal treatment to various degree. The advantages of Chinese herbal medicine in preventing and controlling epidemics have been highlighted, and a wide range of effective prescriptions and herbal medicines have been widely used.

As a special commodity for the prevention, diagnosis, and treatment of diseases, herbal medicines are closely related to people's immediate interests and social harmony and stability. However, in the current market environment, it is difficult to ensure the quality of medicinal herbs due to some illegal business, processing and adulteration problems.

In February 2016, six batches of Saint John's Wort products manufactured in 2013 and sold in the UK were recalled due to higher levels of pyrrolizidine alkaloids (PAs) than recommended by the European Medicines Agency. Authorities had difficulty determining the source of the adulterated material and where the incriminated batches ended.

A study by Booker et al. (Booker et al., 2018) of the quality of herbal products on the market found that some samples contained undeclared edible dyes. The concentrations of active ingredients in the samples were much lower than those of high-quality herbs.

Herbal products are susceptible to heavy metal contamination, especially in rapidly developing countries such as China and India. Pollution from heavy industry is a particular problem, as some plants naturally accumulate heavy metals, which severely affects the quality of herbal medicines. We need to regulate the environment in which herbs are cultivated.

In order to ensure the quality of herbal medicine, it is necessary to understand the factors that affect its quality and to propose new solutions. What technology can solve these problems with herbs? The emergence of blockchain technology quickly attracted people's attention. Driven by both policy and market demand, blockchain technology is rapidly expanding in the medical field. Blockchain technology can be used to track the whole process of herbal medicine production, processing and sales, which perfectly fits with the supply chain system and increases the control ability of herbal medicine products. Each block on the blockchain has a timestamp to form a chain. From the production, processing, transportation, and sale of herbs, the chronological transactions form a complete record of the whole process.

The immutable and decentralised characteristics of the blockchain can increase credit endorsement. The nodes on the chain are able to supervise each other. Moreover, due to too much information uploaded to the chain, it also increases the risk and difficulties of falsification. Blockchain technology can also reduce supply chain costs. It establishes connections to various links in the supply chain to optimise the supply chain of herbal products, which can reduce unnecessary double-validation and thus improve efficiency.

Using blockchain technology can better clarify responsibilities and strengthen credit registries. Once there is a problem with which link, it is easy to locate the responsible unit and the corresponding responsible person after the incident. It will be much more difficult for fakes to pass off as good products.

The herbal medicine base cultivation chain includes seedlings, irrigation water, soil, air, and other key factors that affect the quality of herbal medicine. A great deal of practical experience has shown that the better seedling variety is selected, the better quality of the herbs. The quality of herbs can vary greatly depending on the environment and climatic conditions in which they are grown. By recording these growth conditions and other information on the chain, a traceable record of the entire herbal production process can be made, which facilitates finding the causes that affect the quality of the batch of herbs. Since the data that exists on the chain is typically structured, it aids in data analysis. If this information is studied, it is more able to find out the growth patterns of the herbs from which better and higher quality herbs can be cultivated. We want to take advantage of the immutable nature of the blockchain to document these critical factors and enable nodes in the chain to share this information. In this herbal medicine quality and safety supervisory model (Liu, Peng, Luo, Tang, & Liu, 2021), the main focus is on the traceability of the production records of herbal medicines. Figure 5.9 shows a flowchart of information collection and uploading of herbal medicine production. For example, the name of herbal medicine, the person in charge of the area and the brand of fertilizer can be input into the supervisory system. Some information such as temperature, humidity, image information and geographical location can be automatically collected by the system through sensors. Each sensor has a wireless data transmitting module and data storage module, which can send the collected data in real-time.

The blockchain-based quality and safety management model of Chinese herbal medicine can monitor and track the data generated from the production to sales of Chinese herbal medicine in real-time and process it accordingly. This article is based on the Fabric framework introduced by IBM for system development. Use Docker container and a shell script to build and configure the blockchain network, use Go language to write related smart contracts and back-end servers, and use Vue as the front-end

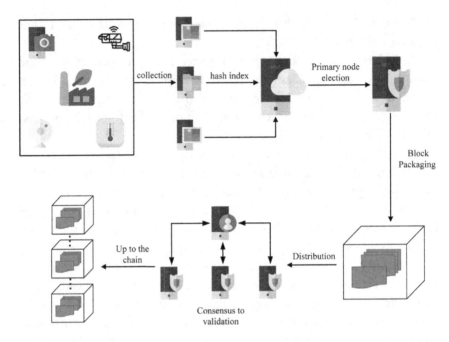

FIGURE 5.9 The process of uploading herbal production information to the blockchain.

framework to provide users with corresponding front-end web pages for operation. The schematic diagram of the system architecture is shown in Figure 5.10.

The application layer is mainly used by the participating users of the platform in the form of a Web browser. Different user rights are different, and the data operation rights are strictly divided to ensure the independence and security of information.

The service layer is for business application developers. Based on a distributed ledger, it supports business-related functional modules such as chain code, secret key management, and transactions, and provides a higher level of application development support.

The storage layer includes two parts: on-chain storage and off-chain storage. Almost all blockchain systems, especially blockchain applications that integrate with the real economy and the real world, require on-chain and off-chain collaboration. The use of off-chain databases by enterprises can facilitate operations, such as, data backup management, and on-chain data can ensure that enterprise data will not be tampered with.

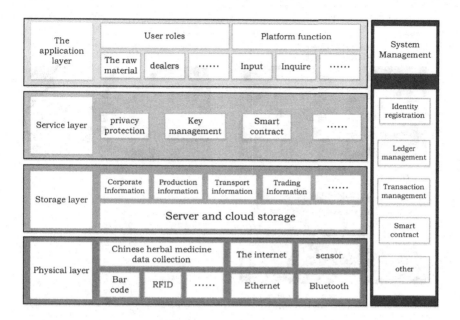

FIGURE 5.10   Overall architecture of the system.

The physical layer completes the recording of the actual status of Chinese herbal medicines in the actual production and circulation process by using RFID, two-dimensional codes, and so on and uploads them to the system through the network.

System management mainly performs functions such as identity audit and verification of platform nodes, management of accounts and transactions, user/role authority management, and platform operation and maintenance.

The product packaging produced on the basis of the Chinese herbal medicine quality and safety management platform has a unique traceable barcode or QR code. When consumers use their mobile phones to scan the identification code on the packaging bag, they can quickly query the information stored on the blockchain network. Figure 5.11 is an example of a blockchain-based Chinese herbal medicine quality and safety management model. Consumers can obtain the production and traceability information of the product by scanning the QR code or barcode on the product package through the mini program. 5.11(a) and (b) show detailed information on Chinese herbal medicine production and the data on the chain. Consumers can view the corresponding production, processing, and transportation

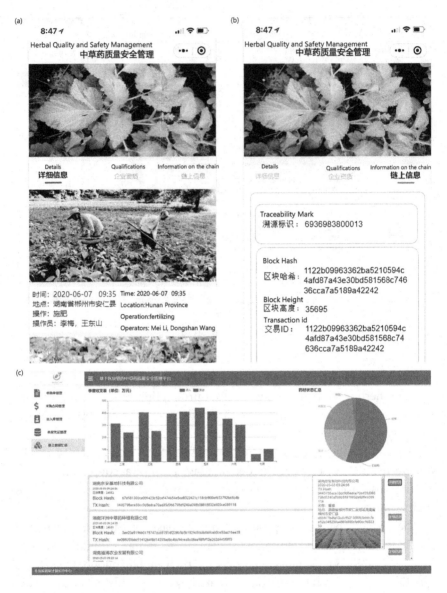

FIGURE 5.11   System working interface.

information of the purchased product through the mini program. The system uses the non-tampering feature of the blockchain network to ensure that consumers view the

Figure 5.11c is the interface for enterprise-level users to use the blockchain-based Chinese herbal medicine quality and safety management platform. The company can use this platform to initiate transactions with cooperating units. The transaction contract and object information will be recorded on the chain to facilitate the review of the regulatory agency and to reduce corruption within the enterprise. Enterprises can only view public information on the chain and information that has been authorised to view. Unauthorised information cannot be viewed, and only the encrypted hash value of unauthorised information can be viewed.

5.8 VGUARD: A SPATIOTEMPORAL EFFICIENCY DOUBLE-LEVEL BLOCKCHAIN METHOD FOR VACCINE PRODUCTION SUPERVISION

A vaccine is a biological product which is an important means for human beings to protect themselves. Most of its users are young children with weak immunity. Once a vaccine has a problem, it will pose a serious threat to the lives of many people. At present, the supervision of vaccine production is very rough. The vaccine production record is completely controlled by the enterprises. Enterprises only submit production records to the supervisory agency for review when the vaccine needs to be sold. Production records are easily forged and modified.

In order to solve the shortcomings of traditional centralised management. We propose a supervision method for vaccine production based on double-level blockchain (Hu, Peng, Long, Jiang, & Wei, 2019).

At first, we have designed a double-level blockchain structure. The first level is private data of vaccine production enterprise, including the production records and corresponding hash. The next level is public data, including the production records hash and vaccine information. In this way, we make vaccine enterprise to submit production records in a timely manner without fear of privacy leaks. We avoid enterprise tampering or falsification of production records through the non-tampering features and time stamps of the blockchain.

To improve time efficiency, we propose a consensus mechanism for multi-node cooperation. The primary supervisory node provides sorting services and verifies the correctness of the blockchain replica. The ordinary supervisory node can replace the primary supervisory node when necessary, and help the primary supervisory node recovers data in case of information loss. The review node is responsible for providing complete and correct blockchain copies for other nodes. So we can avoid the problem of waste of time resources in the traditional blockchain system.

In addition, in order to avoid the waste of space caused by the redundancy of the blockchain, we propose a vaccine data cutting mechanism. We use the timestamp of the blockchain and the vaccine validity period to determine if the block can be cut. At the same time, it is also possible to judge whether the block can be cut based on the information exchange with the vaccination institution.

Through these methods, we have realised spatiotemporal efficiency supervision of vaccine production. And for the time being, research work in the field of vaccine production supervision is still very rare. So our work is groundbreaking.

5.8.1 Background

Vaccine is considered one of the greatest public health achievements in the 20th century. It can prevent diseases and be said to directly affect people's health. Once the vaccine has a problem, it can cause serious harm to the vaccinator's body. The problem vaccine will also make the vaccinator unable to resist many infectious diseases. These diseases can harm the health of patients and even cause death. In addition, there are many young children and infants among the users of the vaccine. They are weakly resistant and need a safer vaccination.

However, in recent years, the vaccine industries, which should be strictly supervised, has experienced many accidents. The vaccination incident of Changchun Changsheng Bio-Technology company shocked the country. The Shandong problem vaccine case is affected in 24 provinces or cities. Shanxi's invalid vaccine has caused nearly 100 children to die, maiming, or serious illness.

These incidents have caused enormous harm. Vaccine production requires deeper supervision.

A typical supervisory method of vaccine production is shown in Figure 5.12. First, the FDA is responsible for determining the list of vaccine lot release agency. Second, the local FDA is responsible for assisting the local vaccine lot release agency to carry out the vaccine lot release work. When a vaccine enterprise applies to the local vaccine lot release agency for vaccine lot release, the vaccine lot release agency verifies the production records and vaccine samples submitted by the vaccine enterprise. If the vaccine is qualified, the vaccine lot release agency will issue a lot of release certification to the enterprise.

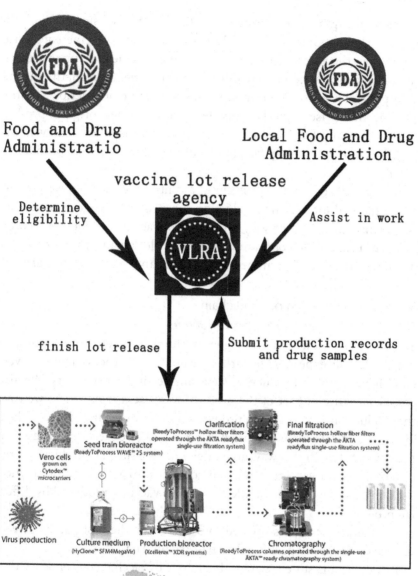

FIGURE 5.12 Vaccine production, review, and marketing process.

There are quite a few problems with this type of supervision. The vaccine production record is fully managed by the vaccine enterprise. Only when the vaccine needs to be sold, the vaccine enterprise submits the vaccine production records. In this management model, the vaccine enterprise can make some modifications to their production records. Vaccine enterprises can also completely destroy their original production records and fabricate new production records. They can even create a batch of vaccines by way of blending and make a fake production record.

In order to address the problem of a centralised method, we propose a new method for vaccine production supervision. It enables decentralised management and privacy protection of vaccine production records. Vaccine production records are stored on the blockchain. The vaccine production time can be determined by the timestamp on the blockchain.

5.8.2 Specific Design of Blockchain

5.8.2.1 Double-Layer Blockchain Structure

The vaccine production undergoes a number of different steps and potency testing experiments during the producing process. Different vaccines have different production steps and testing experiments. We also consider testing as part of the production process steps. Then, we treat the production record of each production step as a separate piece of data. This piece of data holds the production record or experimental result of the current step. In this way, no matter what the specific production process of a certain vaccine is, we can connect it to a series of production data. In this way, we can handle the various vaccines produced by different processes.

The storage of data is divided into two parts, the first part is private data, and the second part is public blockchain data.

Private data is stored in a local database of vaccine enterprises. Other nodes within the blockchain do not have access to it. The specific content of the private data is shown in Table 5.1. Its main content is the production

TABLE 5.1　Private Data Storage Structure

Production record 1	Record time 1	Hash	Start signal
Production record 2	Record time 2	Hash	Previous hash

TABLE 5.2   Blockchain Data Storage Structure

Block head	Block number	Timestamp
	Hash	Previous block hash
	Review node signature	Enterprise signature
	Vaccine name	Validity period
	Lot release numbering	Supervisory node signature
Transaction	Hash	Previous transaction hash
	Enterprise signature	Timestamp

records, the time when the production record is generated and the corresponding hash.

Public blockchain data is mainly divided into two parts. One is the block head data, and the other is a lot of transactions. The specific data structures are shown in Table 5.2.

The header data of the block mainly includes the block number (that is, the block height, indicating how many blocks are currently included in the blockchain), the timestamp, the signature of the enterprise and the vaccine name (used to determine the vaccine production time and the enterprise production capacity), the hash value of the block and the hash value of the previous block (to prevent the block data from being tampered with), the validity period of the vaccine and lot release numbering (for cutting the block), and the signatures of the review and supervisory nodes.

One block represents a batch of vaccines, with multiple transactions in each block. Each transaction in the block represents a process for each batch of vaccine in the production process. The hash of the transaction is the encryption of the production record of this production process. Each transaction also has its own timestamp and signature of the production enterprise, as well as the hash value of the previous transaction (previous production process) to prevent production data fraud.

Based on the traditional blockchain structure, we redesign the data structure for the vaccine production process. The current structure is a blockchain structure that is specifically adapted to the supervision of vaccine production. This structure stores the enterprise's privacy data and hash data separately, protecting the process of privacy of the enterprise's production of vaccines. In addition, uploading the hash also ensures that the real data will not be tampered with. With this structure, enterprises can safely upload data to the review nodes instantly. This method guarantees the authenticity of the production records of the enterprise while guaranteeing the privacy of the production of the enterprise.

5.8.2.2 Consensus Mechanism for Multi-Node Cooperate

We maintain the consistency of the blockchain replica through the sorting service provided by the primary supervisory node. The primary supervisory node receives the blocks from each of review nodes. It arranges the blocks in the order in which they are received. It then broadcasts the blocks in turn to the blockchain network. Each node will receive the blocks sorted by the primary supervisor node. These nodes again judge whether the received blocks are in the correct order based on the hash value and the previous block hash value saved by the received block. In this way, it can be ensured that the replica of the blockchain held by each node is a sorted blockchain by the primary supervisory nodes. This method ensures the consistency of the blockchain replica saved by each node and avoids the occurrence of forks. At the same time, this method also avoids problems such as low time efficiency and waste of resources caused by traditional blockchain consensus mechanisms such as proof of work.

All nodes in the blockchain network can verify whether there is a problem with their own blockchain replica by accessing the primary supervisory node or review nodes. If a node does not receive a complete replica of the blockchain or saves an incorrect replica of the blockchain, it can connect to the primary supervisory node and then download the complete and correct replica of the blockchain.

When there is a problem with the primary supervisory node, the function can be replaced by an ordinary supervisory node. If the primary supervisory node is invalid, it can delegate one ordinary supervisory node to replace it. If the primary supervisory node has problems such as data loss, it can connect to all ordinary supervisory nodes; it then selects a consistent blockchain replica saved by most of ordinary supervisory nodes to download and save.

The way to verify the correctness of the blockchain replica and the way to recover the data are shown in Figure 5.13. The arrows of the primary supervisory node and ordinary supervisory nodes are mainly used to ensure the reliability of the blockchain. The arrows between ordinary enterprise nodes and review nodes and the arrows between them and the primary supervisory node are mainly used to verify and download correct and complete data.

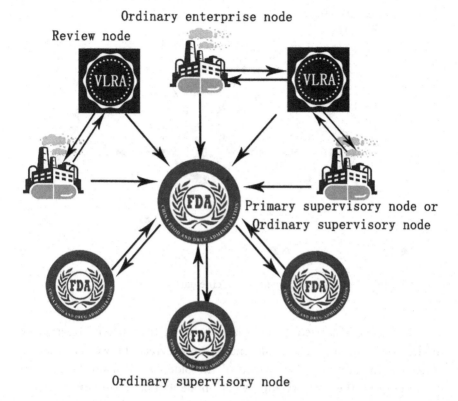

FIGURE 5.13   Vaccine production, review, and marketing process.

5.8.2.3 Cutting Mechanism Based on Timestamp and Information Interaction

To cut unwanted blocks, first, the supervisor node will set a cut flag for each block.

As shown in Figure 5.14, in both cases, the supervisor node sets the cutting flag of the block to require cutting. First, the time when the vaccine represented by the block reached the expiration date was detected. In this case, the node will compare the current time with the validity period of the vaccine stored in the block to determine whether the batch of vaccines has exceeded the validity period. Second, the vaccination agency sends information to a supervisory node through the application software. The supervisory node judges that the vaccine represents by a certain block has been used according to the received information, and then sets the cutting flag of the block should be cut.

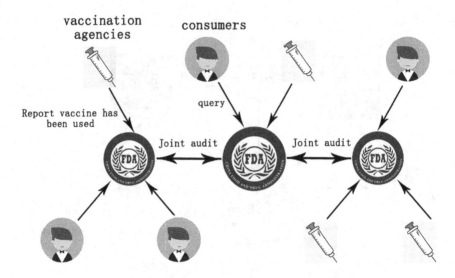

FIGURE 5.14 Cutting mechanism for vaccine data.

Audit work is carried out regularly between the various supervisory nodes. At this point, the saved cut marks are integrated between the nodes. After the integration is completed, if the oldest part of the blockchain should be cut, the primary supervisory node will broadcast to the entire network. The node that receives the broadcast cuts the blockchain replica that it has saved. For auditing purposes, we recommend that the primary supervisory node still maintains the most complete blockchain data.

In this way, we can ensure that the production source of vaccine that needs to be used, can be verified, while removing unnecessary redundant information. This cutting mechanism can effectively control the size of the blockchain and avoid excessive space requirements.

5.8.3 Specific Design of the System

5.8.3.1 Specific Process of vGuard

We first built a blockchain network. As shown in Figure 5.15, according to the real vaccine supervision process, we divide the nodes participating in the blockchain into four categories: ordinary enterprise nodes, review nodes, ordinary supervisory nodes, and primary supervisory node. At the same time, our network will interact with consumers and vaccination agencies.

The primary supervisory node issues certificates for each node in turn, so that these node can join the blockchain system. All nodes are

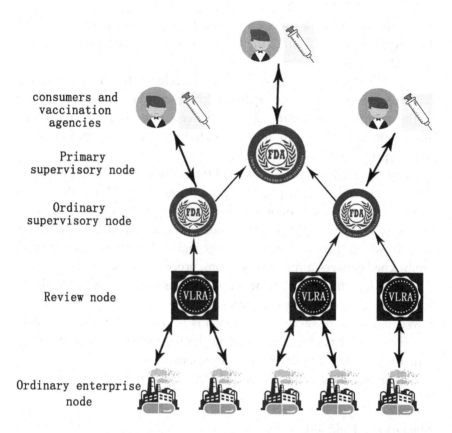

FIGURE 5.15   Composition of vGuard.

connected to the primary supervisor node. The ordinary enterprise node finds each review node by asking the primary supervisory node and then selects some review nodes to establish a connection.

To further ensure that the production of each batch of vaccine is real, we add the embedded equipment to the first equipment (such as bioreactors) that should be used in the production of vaccines. The device sends a hash to the review nodes and the enterprise nodes when the machine is booted.

Then, vaccine enterprises begin to produce a batch of vaccine. When a production process is completed, the staff needs to save the production record. Production records are saved to the vaccine enterprise's local database, they will also save the timestamp when each production record is generated. Next, the worker hashes the production record. The production record hash and time stamp, the hash of the previous process record, and so on constitute a transaction, and broadcast to the review nodes. The previous process hash of the first transaction is the hash send by the embedded device.

To further protect the privacy of the vaccine enterprise's producing process, we allow vaccine enterprises to send some extra-transactions.

The purpose of these transactions is to keep the number of transactions in each block consistent. In this way, we hide the number of process steps an enterprise produces for a vaccine.

These transactions, just like normal transactions, have their own hash, timestamps, and hash of previous production record. The difference is that the hash of these transactions is not generated by a specific production record but by a random string chosen by the vaccine enterprise. The order in which these transactions are generated is random. They may be sandwiched between any two production process transactions.

In addition, the content of these transactions used for hashing will also be submitted to the review agency for review.

When a batch of vaccine production is completed, the vaccine enterprise sends a lot release application to the review node. The application contains the final transaction, i.e., a lot release transaction.

You can see the specific operation of this process in Algorithm 1.

Algorithm 1 Production

```
1: equipment.get(hash)
2: hash → Review node
3: hash → Current node
4: // Send start signal
5: equipment.get(data)
6: equipment.get(time)
7: // After finished production step 1
8: // Get production data and time
9: data → Local database
10: time → Local database
11: // Save the first data
12: transaction.hash ← SHA256(data)
13: transaction.prehash ← hash
14: transaction.time ← time1
```

15: transaction.signature ← enterprise.signature()
16: transaction → Review node
17: // Form a transaction
18: // And send to review node
19:....
20: creatapply(vaccine name, period, last transaction)
21: apply → Review node
22: local database →Review node
23: // Enterprise submit application

You can also see the visual representation of this process in Figure 5.16.

The vaccine enterprise issue a lot of release application and submit production records and vaccine samples. The review node finds all relevant transactions from the transaction pool based on the hash of the previous

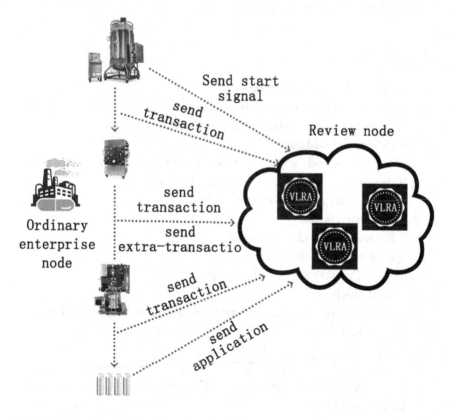

FIGURE 5.16   Production process and consistent transaction quantity principle.

transaction saved in the transaction. Then it packages all transactions and related information (Such as vaccine name, expiration date, etc.) into one block.

The review node begins to check the production records and vaccine samples provided by the vaccine enterprise. They also need to check whether the hash of the submitted production records is consistent with the hash of the intra-block transaction.

If this batch of vaccine passes the review, the review node needs to write the corresponding lot release number to the block. In addition, the review node also needs to sign the block with its own private key.

The review node sends the block to the primary supervisor node. The primary supervisory node checks the block. If the check is successful, the primary supervisory node signs the block. Finally, it broadcasts block sequentially to the entire network.

We describe this process in Algorithm 2.

Algorithm 2 Review

1: review node.get(transaction)
2: // The review node finds all transactions from the transaction pool
3: // By previous transaction hash saved per transaction
4: review node.get(data)
5: // The review node get production data from enterprise
6: review node.creatblock(transactions, blockhead)
7: if SHA256(data)!=transaction.hash
8: then Return false
9: // Review node audit block data
10: review node.signature(block)
11: block → Primary supervisory node
12: // Send block
13: if(block.enterprise signature.error()||block.review signature.error())
14: then Return false
15: primary node.signature(block)
16: block → Blockchain network
17: // Check the block and sign it. Then broadcast the block to the Blockchain network
18: Return true

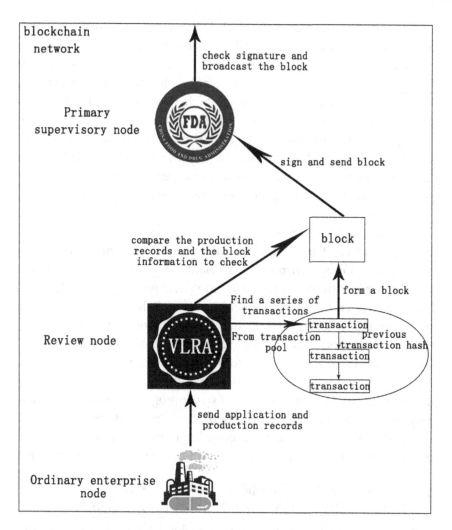

FIGURE 5.17   Review process.

You can see the visual representation of the process in Figure 5.17.

When consumers need to verify the reliability of the vaccine, they can connect to the supervisory node responsible for the area by scanning the barcode on the vaccine bottle. The supervisory node sends back the query result through the saved blockchain replica (Return true if the batch of vaccine information is saved in the blockchain). If the search result is true, the vaccine is a validated vaccine, otherwise, the vaccine may be problematic.

Using the transparency of the blockchain, we encourage ordinary enterprise nodes to check the data stored on the blockchain. They can query the timestamps on each block and the timestamps of transactions within the block, vaccine enterprises in various blocks and vaccines represented by each block. Based on these, they judge whether the production capacity of a certain vaccine enterprise is in an abnormal state. If there is a problem, they can report to the supervisory node. Once the report is verified, the supervisory agency will give the reported enterprise a certain reward. At the same time, the supervisory agency will also impose penalties on the illegal enterprises, including invalidating their certificates, and other realistic penalties.

5.8.3.2 System Implementation

We implemented vGuard based on Fabric framework which provided by IBM. Our operating environment is Ubuntu 18.04 The Docker container was also used for the development of our system prototype. We use nodejs for backend development and writing business logic (such as writing smart contracts). As shown in Figure 5.18, we provide different programs for different nodes. These include management pages for primary supervisory node, WeChat application for users and vaccination agencies, and management pages for review nodes. In addition, it also includes some management applications and related server programs. We also use these programs to systematically test the method we design. These tests are used to evaluate the performance of our completed systems and to demonstrate that our design method is fully applicable to current vaccine production.

5.9 GEOAI-BASED EPIDEMIC CONTROL WITH GEO-SOCIAL DATA SHARING ON BLOCKCHAIN

Epidemics especially those caused by major contagious diseases have entailed huge losses in human history. The fights have thus never stopped to prevent pandemics. Due to its acute outbreak, is generally susceptible to the population regardless of ages, so strict quarantine of the infections becomes the most effective means for epidemic control, which has been proved in the prevention of other contagious diseases, such as SARS and H1N1. The key strategy are widely used to find infected and suspected patients is still the epidemiological tracking of confirmed cases. However, this may fail to identify infections especially when patients do not show any symptoms. Therefore, the approach to rapid, effective, and simple infection identification is essential to prevent the spread of a contagious disease.

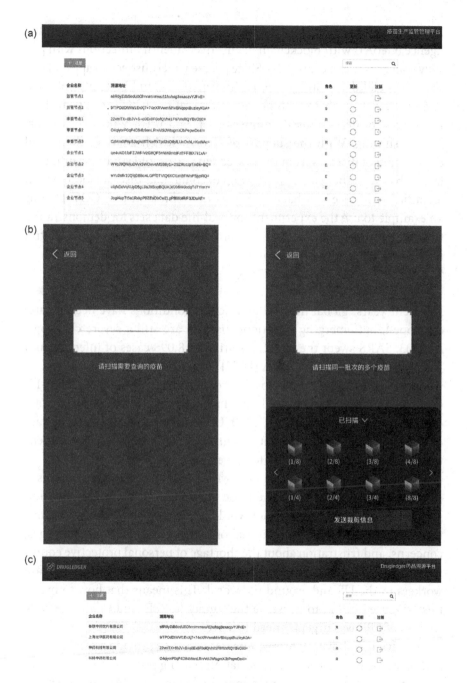

FIGURE 5.18 A system we have developed specifically for the vGuard.

This paper proposes to leverage social apps and Geospatial artificial intelligence (GeoAI) with Blockchain to effectively identify infections with privacy concerns (Peng et al. 2021). Since people widely use social apps, a large scale of social data with geospatial information could be easily collected and kept on Blockchain with privacy preservation, which thus provides a framework of decentralised, tamper-proof, and privacy-preserved information sharing. With the support of GeoAI, which analyses the spatial distribution of diseases from the shared data, we could study the influence factors based on the spatial propagation of contagious diseases for infection identification. Since WeChat is widely used in China, we take COVID-19 as an example to use the experiments on real-life data sets for demonstrating the effectiveness of our method, and provide insight into epidemic control in terms of geo-social data sharing.

5.9.1 Background

In recent years, global medical and health conditions have been greatly developed, but emerging infectious diseases are still a severe challenge. In 2003, SARS swept the world, resulting in 8,098 cases of infection and 774 deaths. In 2009, influenza A (H1N1) caused over 18,500 deaths worldwide. Since the outbreak of novel coronavirus pneumonia (COVID-19) occurred in 2019, it has infected over 4 million people with about 300,000 deaths word wide by May 10th, 2020. Up to now, there is no cure or vaccine for COVID-19. Therefore, it is of great importance to effectively identify suspected patients in order to prevent epidemics.

However, the identification of novel contagious diseases remains a challenge, and how to overcome these difficulties for rapid, effective and simple identification of infections would be the key to the control of contagious diseases. The online editorial of JAMA recognises the challenges, concerns, and frustration about the shortage of personal protective equipment (PPE) that is affecting the care of patients and safety of health care workers in the US and around the world. This means that how to maximise the use of PPE, to conserve the supply of PPE, and to identify new sources of PPE was urgently need to solve.

To solve the above problems, it is necessary to provide a safe, reliable and privacy-preserved social information sharing platform to understand the social dynamics. Therefore, a model of infectious disease prevention and control based on social applications and GeoAI is proposed in terms of Geo-Social data sharing on Blockchain. At the same time, this article also takes Chinese mobile social app WeChat as an example, Under the influence of the COVID-19, it is leveraged to enable users easily to share their social data on Blockchain with privacy control, so as to realise the analysis and control of the epidemics by combining GeoAI techniques and infectious disease dynamic model.

5.9.2 Proposed Model

5.9.2.1 Network Overview

In the GeoAI-based epidemic control system with geo-social data sharing on Blockchain, users are able to upload and receive information. The network structure of the system is shown in Figure 5.19.

Figure 5.19 shows that the Blockchain of epidemic information sharing is composed of three parts: users, medical institutions, and GeoAI analysis system. A user is able to report daily health information and trajectories, and to apply for reasoning his possibility of infection. A medical institution diagnoses whether a user is infected, tracks the confirmed patients, records and publishes the confirmed patients over the network with privacy protection. The GeoAI system is introduced to analyse the daily health information uploaded by users and the travel histories of the confirmed cases on the Blockchain, so as to judge whether a user is a suspected patient who are able to request testing. Meanwhile, the confirmed patient trajectory distribution published by the medical institution is visually displayed on the map in order to caution other social users.

5.9.2.2 Proposed System

The system is based on social apps, GeoAI, Blockchain, and the infectious disease dynamics model. Blockchain provides a privacy-preserved data

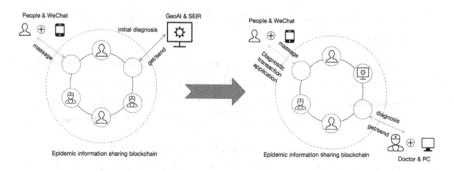

FIGURE 5.19   The network structure.

infrastructure, GeoAI is built on the Blockchain network to process and analyse the data in order to enable the analysis of epidemics.

The workflow of GeoAI is as follows:

1. Data collection. After processing, the data such as trajectories and physical examination details reported by users are collected and stored in the network. Meanwhile, the symptom information and distribution map of confirmed patients are collected. Different types of basic data provide training data for machine learning or deep learning models to train the relationship between the distribution of patients, trajectories and the environment in epidemics.

2. Model construction. Based on the training data generated in the process of data preparation, the neural network model was trained. Meanwhile, the model was continuously evaluated iteratively through verification and testing, and the distribution, trajectory and physical conditions of patients are combined with the real environment to achieve the accuracy requirements for practical application.

3. Model application. Model publishing and application is the ultimate goal of the spatial machine learning workflow. In the form of tools or services, the model obtained by training is used to calculate and analyse data to obtain accurate distribution of epidemic patients.

5.9.2.3 Data Analysis by GeoAI

The GeoAI module compares the symptoms and distribution areas of the confirmed patients, determines whether a user is a suspected patient, and feeds back the information to the users. The specific process is as follows:

1. Collect daily health information M_H and travel histories M_T uploaded by users;

2. Compare the physical status information of confirmed patients, M'_H, with the distribution of M'_T in the region of a user. Among them, the higher the similarity between M_H and M'_H, the higher probability of infection, and so does to the coincidence between M_T and M'_T;

3. If the user is a suspected patient, the user would be notified to stay at home to avoid the spread of disease, waiting for a testing and medical care from the medical institution.

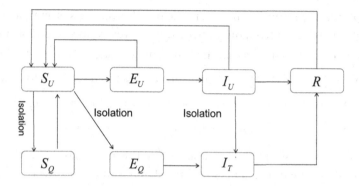

FIGURE 5.20 Dynamics model of infectious disease.

The SEIR infectious disease dynamics model in the GeoAI system module is shown in Figure 5.20.

In the Blockchain, nodes can be divided into four types: S is the susceptible group, E is the asymptomatic group, I is the infected group, and R is the recovered group. And R can be converted to S to some extent.

In the Figure 5.20, U means not quarantined, Q means quarantined, and T means quarantined in a hospital. S_U is the susceptible person who is not quarantined, S_Q is the susceptible person who is quarantined, E_U is the asymptomatic person who is not quarantined, E_Q is the asymptomatic person who is quarantined, I_U is the infected person who is not quarantined, I_T is the infected person who is quarantined in the hospital, and R is the recovered person.

In this model, all individuals have the probability of infection, and some of them have strong physical quality and can recover on their own, but the recovered people can be infected again after recovery. We assume that the probability of the recovered people becoming susceptible is α. Also consider the prevention and treatment of infectious diseases in the process will be taken isolation measures. Therefore, compared with the SEIR kinetic model, S_Q is added to our model to represent the susceptible person in isolation, E_Q represents the asymptomatic person in isolation, and I_T represents the infected person in isolation in the hospital.

Suppose the ratio of quarantine is q, the infection rate was β, the contact probability was ε. The conversion rates of susceptible S_U to the quarantined susceptible S_Q, the quarantined asymptomatic E_Q, and the asymptomatic E_U were respectively as: $\varepsilon q = (1 - \beta)$, $\varepsilon q \beta$, $\varepsilon (1 - q)\beta$. At the same time, considering the influence of unquarantined infected person I_U and asymptomatic person E_U on susceptible people's S_U, the susceptible person S_Q that was released from quarantine was converted to susceptible person S_U again. Here, it assumes that the transmission rate of the lurk to the susceptible is θ, and λ is the rate of quarantine release. Here, $\lambda = \dfrac{1}{4}$ (quarantine for 14 days) is taken. Therefore, the governing equation of susceptible population is: $\dfrac{dS_U}{dt} = -[\varepsilon\beta + \varepsilon q(1-\beta)]S_U(I_U + \theta E_U) + \lambda S_Q + \alpha R$.

For the sake of simplicity, we assume that the lurker has the same spread probability as the infected person, $\theta = 1$. At the same time, we assume that δ is the rate of transformation from lurk to infected person, and take $\delta = \dfrac{1}{7}$ (incubation period of 7 days), μ is the rate of quarantine of the infected person, σ is the recovery rate of the infected person, τ is the mortality rate, ς is the rate of transformation from the quarantined lurk to the quarantined infected person, and ω is the recovery rate of the quarantined infected person.

Then the equation of propagation dynamics is as follows:

$$
\begin{cases}
\dfrac{dS_U}{dt} = \varepsilon\beta + \varepsilon q(1-\beta)S_U(I_U + \theta E_U) + \lambda S_Q + \alpha R \\[2mm]
\dfrac{dE_U}{dt} = \varepsilon\beta(1-q)S_U(I_U + \theta E_U) - \delta E_U \\[2mm]
\dfrac{dI_U}{dt} = \delta E_U - (\mu + \sigma + \tau)I_U \\[2mm]
\dfrac{dS_Q}{dt} = \varepsilon q(1-\beta)S_U(I_U + \theta E_U) - \lambda S_Q - \lambda R \\[2mm]
\dfrac{dE_Q}{dt} = \varepsilon\beta q S_U(I_U + \theta E_U) - \delta E_U \\[2mm]
\dfrac{dI_T}{dt} = \mu I_U + \varsigma E_U - (\tau + \omega)I_T \\[2mm]
\dfrac{dR}{dt} = \sigma I_U + \omega I_T
\end{cases}
\tag{5.1}
$$

5.9.3 The System Based on WeChat-GeoAI on the Blockchain

5.9.3.1 Proposed System and the Flow Chart

People upload personal health information and itinerary to the blockchain through WeChat. The GeoAI-SEIR system will initially analyse the user's

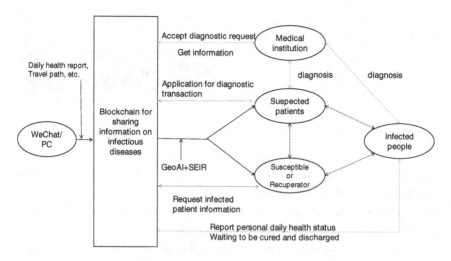

FIGURE 5.21   Flow chart of the system.

health. When the user knows that he is a suspected patient, he can initiate a confirmed transaction application through the blockchain. Other users self-warn themselves by knowing the location, trajectory, and health of the infected person. The flow chart of the system based on WeChat-GeoAI on the Blockchain is shown in Figure 5.21.

5.9.3.2 Initialisation and Registration Phase

The detailed procedures for the initialisation and registration of the system are as follows:

1. Through Hyperledger fabric, the data sharing Blockchain of the prevention and control system is constructed and the gRPC service is initialised.

2. After authorisation by the WeChat client, a user invokes the certificate service (CA) through the SDK, initiates the application of the Blockchain, and obtains the identity certificate.

3. After the Blockchain network receives the registration application, it determines the legitimacy of the user and return the identity certificate, as well as the private-public key pair *SK* and *PK*.

After successful registration, the node information of the user node in the blockchain is shown in Figure 5.22, where the block header includes

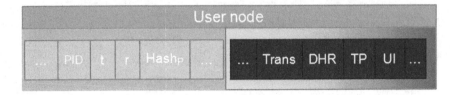

FIGURE 5.22   User authorisation login interface.

user id *PID*, timestamp *t*, random number *r*, hash value of the previous block *Hash_p*, and so on the block body contains all diagnosed patients Transaction information *Trans*, user's daily health report *DHR*, travel path *TP*, user's infection *UI* and other information.

Users upload the daily health status and trajectories to the Blockchain for collection and analysis by GeoAI system.

5.9.3.3 To Initiate a Transaction Application for Confirmation of Suspected Patients

In this stage, if the user receives the feedback information after GeoAI analysis as a suspected patient, the user are suggested to request a confirmation testing application, the medical institution would check the suspected patient after receiving the transaction application, and if the patients are confirmed, the transaction (confirmation information) will be broadcasted on the Blockchain and the user would be marked as an infection. The specific process is shown in Figure 5.23, in which PK_M and SK_M are public and private keys of medical institutions, PK_S and SK_S are public and public keys of patients to be diagnosed, E stands for encryption, Sign stands for signature, *DHI* stands for daily health survey report, *tra* stands for travel trajectory, and *message* stands for transaction information of confirmed patients.

1. Users use WeChat clients will use the private key signature after medical institutions of information (is used for medical institutions to confirm whether the information is sent to the medical institutions) with medical institutions public key encryption after daily health survey report and track (data) for detecting blockchain networks via the SDK trading Proposal (to verify or not), trade proposals to logo, a contract with the transaction to invoke the method and parameter information and client signature information sent to the endorsement (Endorser) node.

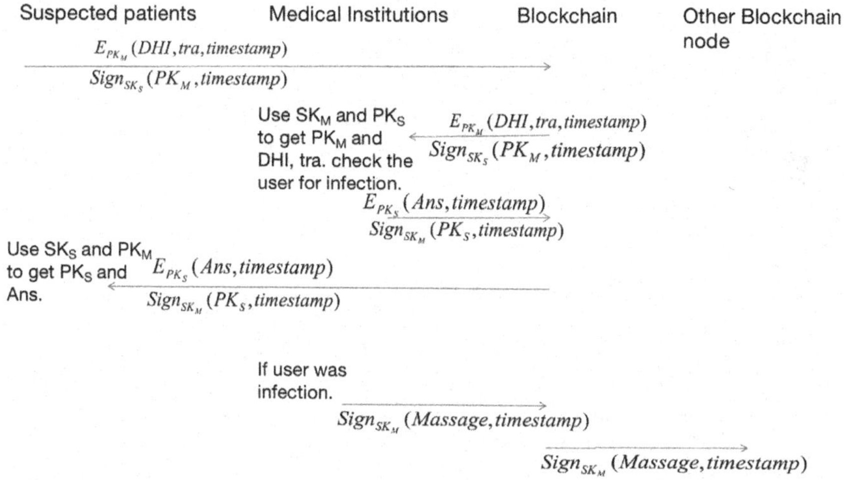

Suspected patients   Medical Institutions   Blockchain   Other Blockchain node

$E_{PK_M}(DHI, tra, timestamp)$

$Sign_{SK_s}(PK_M, timestamp)$

Use SK_M and PK_S to get PK_M and DHI, tra. check the user for infection.

$E_{PK_M}(DHI, tra, timestamp)$

$Sign_{SK_s}(PK_M, timestamp)$

$E_{PK_S}(Ans, timestamp)$

$Sign_{SK_M}(PK_S, timestamp)$

Use SK_S and PK_M to get PK_S and Ans.

$E_{PK_S}(Ans, timestamp)$

$Sign_{SK_M}(PK_S, timestamp)$

If user was infection.

$Sign_{SK_M}(Massage, timestamp)$

$Sign_{SK_M}(Massage, timestamp)$

FIGURE 5.23 Testing flowchart of suspected patients.

2. After the Endorser node receives the transaction Proposal, it verifies the signature and determines whether the submitter has the right to perform the operation. Meanwhile, it simulates the execution of the intelligent contract according to the endorsement strategy, and generates the transaction result based on the current state database execution. The output includes feedback value, read set and write set.

3. Upon receipt of the information returned by the Endorser node, determine whether the result of the proposal is consistent and whether the data should be executed in accordance with the specified endorsement strategy, and submit the data to the medical institution for examination.

4. The medical institution shall verify the health verification transaction of the user, check whether the input and output dependent on the transaction conform to the current state of the blockchain, and record the account book only after the confirmed infected person, and broadcast the disease status of the node submitting the application; otherwise, the transaction is deemed invalid.

5.9.3.4 Distribution of Infectious Diseases under the GeoAI System

After analysis by GeoAI, the epidemic distribution is depicted in this paper. The display diagram in the system is shown in Figure 5.24.

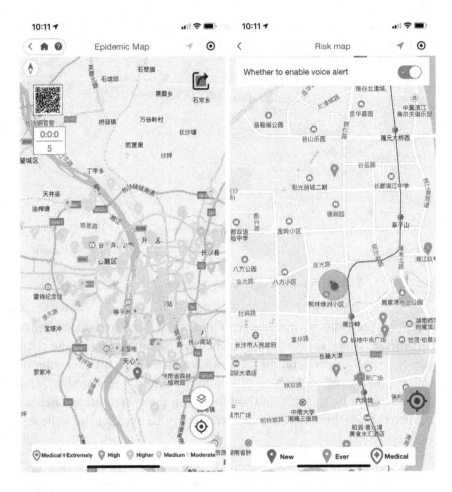

FIGURE 5.24   Epidemic distribution map.

From Figure 5.24, we can clearly obtain the epidemic risk areas, that is, the GeoAI system visualises the distribution of the epidemic, analyses, and determines the epidemic risk areas and displays them, as well as the statistics of the new and old confirmed points, so as to provide certain help for the epidemic prevention and control work of the whole population.

5.10 BLOCKCHAIN DATA SHARING

With the continuous development of Internet technology, the amount of data around the world has exploded. From the user side, almost everyone is now using Internet devices, and with the popularity of the new generation of 5G mobile Internet technology, the amount of data generated by users is growing even more massively. After collecting user data, Internet companies can analyse the data by using advanced data mining and machine learning technologies to guide the behaviour of user applications and provide convenient and intimate services to users. From the service side, the steady and rapid advancement of computer hardware in recent years have led to an abundant supply of powerful computers, data collection devices, and storage media. The development of database and information industry has been greatly facilitated by the update of hardware technology, enabling the storage of large amounts of data and information for transaction management, information retrieval, and data analysis, and many organisations have taken advantage of this cost reduction to create large databases for transaction processing. The knowledge 'mined' from these big data warehouses can be put at the service of the organisations concerned, allowing them to operate efficiently.

However, science and technology is a double-edged sword, while bringing great convenience to human life, the hidden security risks behind big data are not to be underestimated. Both the process of sharing data by users and the process of storing and releasing data for use by the server may generate data privacy issues. With the widespread application of new technologies, such as virtualisation and cloud computing, Internet privacy leaks are commonplace. It has become a hot topic of research to find out how to effectively avoid threats while enjoying the convenience of life in the era of big data.

Blockchain has the characteristics of untamperable and traceable, which can be used in the field of data sharing to ensure that the shared data cannot be tampered with and to ensure the credibility of data storage and sharing. At the same time, blockchain is naturally decentralised and more in line with the application scenarios of data sharing, using blockchain can share file data more efficiently and safely.

The blockchain itself does not have privacy protection features, but using some information security techniques can achieve good privacy protection results. What kind of security technology to combine on the blockchain, and how to combine these security technologies in order to achieve the desired privacy protection when sharing data, this is the blockchain data sharing needs to study the problem.

Blockchain, as a special form of distributed system with data redundancy made to address data immutability, also poses a number of challenges when combined with data sharing. How to make the blockchain and a large number of data-sharing applications combined to make the shared data throughput to a satisfactory level, which is also an important research problem.

5.10.1 Data Security

In June 2013, Edward Snowden, a former CIA employee, exposed the National Security Agency's Prism program, arousing considerable public interest. The Guardian and the Washington Post have revealed that since 2007, the U.S. National Intelligence Agency (NIA) has been able to access the Internet through nine major networks, including Microsoft, Facebook, Google, and Yahoo. The company's central servers in the United States conduct intelligence collection. 'Prism' project monitors the call records of Internet users and their network behaviours and collects the relevant actions of network users and their social networks for intelligence analysis.

The revelation of the 'prism' wiretapping program caused an uproar in public opinion, although Obama repeatedly stressed that the Prism program was designed to combat terrorist attacks and protect national security and had no intention of spying on the privacy of Internet users. It was emphasised that the aim of the expose was that it would not be tolerated that United States intelligence agencies should block Internet freedom and violate the privacy and security of citizens. 'Prism' project once again triggered the issue of how to protect individual privacy.

Traditional cloud storage mainly uses centralised storage as the main mode. However, due to the instability of cloud environment and the highly centralised management architecture design, users' data files often face many security problems and copyright control problems in the cloud. There is a risk of data leakage or direct exposure in the network, which leads to illegal users to obtain data content.

Today, there are a lot of data sharing needs, and protecting data privacy security has become one of the urgent problems to be solved. Failure to address shared data privacy protection may result in the leakage of shared data, or may directly prevent data from being shared. The European Union (EU), composed of 27 member states, is an economic and political union with a range of common policies in different regions. An important area of its cooperation is information sharing on terrorist attacks and criminal activities. However, due to a various security and internal system considerations, many European Union States are reluctant to share their original sensitive data with other members, but to share mining knowledge with other Member States after data mining and processing of the original data.

5.10.2 Blockchain File Storage and Sharing Advantages

At present, the storage system used by Internet enterprises usually takes centralised storage as the main mode. However, due to the centralised characteristics of centralised system, users' data files in these systems are often faced with many security problems and copyright control problems. The risk of data leakage or direct exposure to the network leads to illegal users being able to access the data content and then obtain the important information. At the same time, the centralised system also has a closed nature. When sharing data, the data is completely downloaded to the local through the system centre, which is not as efficient as the decentralised system.

Enterprises adopting centralised storage solutions often don't really use a single high-performance server to provide storage services, because there is a single point of failure for single-server storage. No matter how good the performance of a single server is, it is inevitable that there may be a failure condition, which may be caused by the machine itself or more likely by some occasional program conflict or operational error. Even if the machine is infallible, there will inevitably be an artificial cause for the machine to fail. In this kind of system, once a single machine fails, it needs to be restarted and data recovery may be needed. During this period, the system will be completely unavailable, which is already a terrible experience for the user. What's worse, although a single machine can achieve very high reliability in physical storage, once it fails due to system or software reasons, some data may be lost permanently, which is definitely unacceptable for some important data storage services.

In addition to the problem of single point of failure, single servers have various drawbacks such as limited throughput, poor scalability, and poor scalability. As a result, companies tend to design their systems as distributed systems. Although this approach is a little closer to the decentralised system in form, its essence is still centralised, because the ultimate goal of the whole system to provide services is to make the system look like a single virtual node.

Since we have to use a distributed storage solution, why not combine with blockchain for data storage. Blockchain is naturally a distributed system. If data storage and sharing are carried out in combination with blockchain, it cannot only solve the single point failure problem existing in traditional storage but also improve the throughput. At the same time, the blockchain's immutability can also ensure that data security cannot be tampered with, the blockchain's traceability can achieve effective version control, and the blockchain's decentralised nature can improve the efficiency of data sharing and reduce the communication burden of the backbone network.

5.10.3 Blockchain File Storage and Sharing System Solutions

To build a file storage system based on blockchain, we should first consider where the files are stored. Regardless of the technical details, blockchain technology can be regarded as a tamper-proof decentralised database. Decentralisation is its physical property, and its storage property is unforgeable, while database is its application essence, as we use this technology to store some data. So can our files exist directly on the blockchain as well? It seems that this is completely possible, the earliest blockchain system Bitcoin can only store transaction information, these transactions are essentially structured binary files, only in this application scenario the user submits only transaction data. If we design a blockchain that directly writes files into the system, we can implement the use of blockchain for data storage.

However, the idea of using blockchain for file storage is actually unworkable. Compared with the traditional distributed system, it can be found that, as a distributed system, blockchain needs all the main nodes (mining nodes in bitcoin and Ethereum) to keep complete blockchain data in order to achieve unforgeability. The nodes that do not save complete data can only exist on these master nodes, and their functions are limited. This means that if the files are stored directly in the blockchain, they will be copied to all the primary nodes. This huge amount of redundant distributed storage is acceptable when the amount of data such as transactions is not large, which is why blockchains such as bitcoin and Ethereum can be applied. However, if you need to store such massive data as blockchain files, whether in terms of physical storage or network transmission, it will exert great pressure on the blockchain system. In today's big data era, it is too expensive to implement the redundancy, so almost no blockchain product will store files directly on the blockchain.

The common practice is to store the file on the file system and store the fingerprint of the file and the metadata of the file on the blockchain. File systems can be distributed or centralised. The centralised file system is easy to construct. At present, cloud storage technology can be regarded as a centralised storage system. It needs to combine with the blockchain, and only need to store the locator and file fingerprint of the file storage in the blockchain to complete the most basic blockchain data storage and sharing system. However, as a decentralised system, the centralised file system must be a centralised system controlled in a single enterprise. The combination of the two systems actually reduces the decentralised characteristics of blockchain applications. At the same time, there are still some problems in centralised storage, such as poor scalability and poor scalability. User storage files are still completely dependent on this centralised storage system, which causes great pressure on the backbone network and results in the system throughput is limited.

In summary, it seems that using a distributed storage system to store files, while storing file fingerprints and some metadata on the blockchain, maybe the optimal solution to achieve a combination of blockchain and data-sharing system. The next subsection will give a detailed introduction to this solution of blockchain distributed file-sharing system.

5.10.4 Blockchain Distributed File Storage and Sharing System Case

In this case, the blockchain distributed file system will be divided into a storage layer, a protocol layer, a service layer, and an application layer, as shown in the following Figure 5.25.

5.10.4.1 Storage Layer

The storage layer includes file storage and blockchain data storage. File storage uses a peer-to-peer decentralised network, where the nodes of the peer-to-peer network are a series of anonymous nodes used to store files, which can be individual storage devices, a collective with free storage resources, or a cloud storage provider. The storage layer needs to deal with a series of algorithms and logic for file distribution storage, including file multi-threaded slicing and dicing strategies, file distribution mechanisms, and metadata types. Blockchain data storage is the need for a traditional blockchain, this blockchain needs to have a data interface for the file storage system to store metadata, there are many such blockchain systems, typically a public chain on behalf of ethereum, alliance chain on behalf of Hyperledger Fabric.

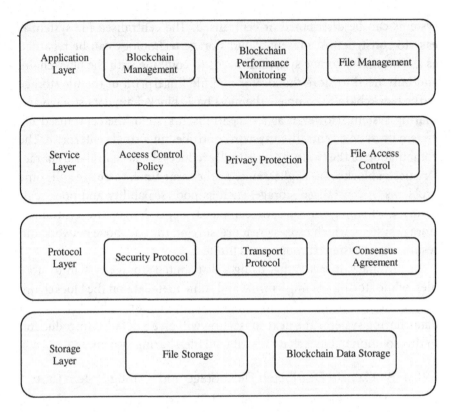

FIGURE 5.25   The architecture of block chain distributed file system.

5.10.4.2 Protocol Layer

The protocol layer contains numerous protocols needed to implement the blockchain distributed file storage and sharing system. Among them, file management needs to include security algorithms, security protocols and transfer protocols, and so on. The files stored in the underlying storage layer need to ensure their security, reliability and consistency, which depends on the operation of each algorithm in the protocol layer. The protocols needed for the blockchain are mainly the identity control protocol in the federated chain, and the consensus protocol.

5.10.4.3 Service Layer

The service layer is an integrated management of the underlying functionality, including the development of access control policies, the specific implementation of privacy protections, the specific management methods for file distribution and file access control, the management of consensus mechanisms, and the management of blockchain smart contracts. These management capabilities are provided as part of the user's own management definitions, and by abstracting the underlying resources and functions, these management capabilities are exposed to upper-level development and use.

5.10.4.4 Application Layer

The corresponding application platform includes a blockchain management module, a blockchain performance monitoring module, an attribute management module, and a file management module.

5.11 CHAPTER SUMMARY

The advantages of blockchain high transparency, distributed bookkeeping and smart contracts will inject new live blood into multi-scenario applications. At a time when the public is increasingly concerned about food and drug safety, the true value of products, and resistance to counterfeit products, with the continuous testing of enterprises in the supply chain field, although the application of blockchain in the supply chain is still in its infancy, believe that its real implementation is just around the corner. The driving forces are as follows:

1. Blockchain's information transparency can improve the overall efficiency of the supply chain upstream and downstream: the use of blockchain technology can make information open between upstream and downstream enterprises. As a result, information such as demand changes can be reflected in real-time to the various entities in the chain, and each enterprise can keep abreast of the progress of logistics in order to take appropriate measures. Similar to the VMI (Vendor Managed Inventory) strategy, this approach enhances the possibility of multi-party collaboration for information visualisation, process optimisation, and demand management to improve the overall efficiency of the system.

2. Blockchain's immutability and transparency reduce the difficulty of regulation: any single transaction operation in the supply chain is permanently recorded on a block and made transparent on the blockchain. Whether it is the monitoring of counterfeit goods, substandard

goods, or the identification of evidence and liability after disputes arise in the supply chain, the intervention of the relevant departments is much simpler, making it easy to solve the problem.

3. The advantages of blockchain in tracking counterfeit and shoddy goods meet the needs of consumers: at present, the sales model of Internet-based products has become more mature, but the quality of products has always been a hot topic of public concern, and counterfeit and shoddy goods on the Internet platform have been criticised by consumers. In the future, enterprises that can make the supply chain transparent and trace the source of counterfeit and shoddy products will be widely recognised by the public.

4. The development of IoT technologies is key: the technologies that currently connect physical products to the network are radio frequency identification, two-dimensional barcodes and near-field communication. On the blockchain, in order to ensure the smooth flow of information, digital tagging is necessary at every stage of logistics in the supply chain and needs to be installed in the moment of operation. How to add digital tags for the purpose of tracking physical products still requires technical solution ideas.

5. Supply chain finance or a current practical solution: enterprises in the supply chain of historical transaction information by blockchain technology to ensure its credibility, which can help financial institutions to quickly assess the creditworthiness of enterprises, reduce the difficulty of financing enterprises, fully reflect the value of enterprises.

In short, blockchain technologies can effectively solve the supply chain industry information transmission lag, low agility and other issues, greatly improve transaction trust, conducive to process optimisation, enhance prediction. At the technical level, the establishment of a system of the Internet of Things is a prerequisite for the combination of blockchain technology and the supply chain of manufacturing enterprises, so industries and enterprises with a higher degree of automation and standardisation are expected to be the first to generate the application of blockchain technology. At the same time, the combination of blockchain technology and supply chain finance deserves further attention. Blockchain with supply chain will create a safe and reliable supply chain system, and governments, enterprises, and individuals will all benefit from this new model.

REFERENCES

Booker, A., Agapouda, A., Frommenwiler, D. A., Scotti, F., Reich, E., & Heinrich, M. J. P. (2018). St John's wort (Hypericum perforatum) products–an assessment of their authenticity and quality. *Phytomedicine, 40*, 158–164.

Hu, X., Peng, S., Long, C., Jiang, H., & Wei, L. (2019). *vGuard: a spatiotemporal efficiency supervision method for vaccine production based on double-level blockchain.* 2019 IEEE International Conference on Bioinformatics and Biomedicine (BIBM), IEEE, 1037–1042.

Huang, W.-Y., Cai, Y.-Z., & Zhang, Y. J. N., (2009). Natural phenolic compounds from medicinal herbs and dietary plants: potential use for cancer prevention. *Nutrition and Cancer, 62*(1), 1–20.

Liu, J., Peng, S., Luo, J., Tang, Z. & Liu, H. (2021). *Segmented encryption: a quality and safety supervisory model for herbal medicine based on blockchain technology.* 2020 IEEE International Conference on E-health Networking, Application & Services (HEALTHCOM), IEEE, Shenzhen, 1–6.

Niazi, M., Yari, F., & Shakarami, A. (2019). A review of medicinal herbs in the lamiaceae family used to treat arterial hypertension. *Entomology and Applied Science Letters, 6*(1), 22–27.

Peng, S., Bai, L., Xiong, L., Qu, Q., Xie, X., & Wang, S. (2021). *GeoAI-based epidemic control with geo-social data sharing on blockchain.* 2020 IEEE International Conference on E-health Networking, Application & Services (HEALTHCOM), IEEE, Shenzhen, 1–6.

Tan, W., Lu, J., Huang, M., Li, Y., Chen, M., Wu, G., Gong, J., Zhong, Z., Xu, Z., & Dang, Y. J. C. m. (2011). Anti-cancer natural products isolated from Chinese medicinal herbs. *Chinese Medicine, 6*(1), 1–15.

Wu, J. A., Attele, A. S., Zhang, L., & Yuan, C.-S. (2001). Anti-HIV activity of medicinal herbs: usage and potential development. *The American Journal of Chinese Medicine, 29*(01), 69–81.

Yang, D., Xu, H., Feng, Z., Meng, L., Long, C., & Peng, S. (2020). *A scheme to optimize roadside parking management by using blockchain technology.* 2020 IEEE 6th International Conference on Computer and Communications (ICCC), IEEE, 2235–2239.

CHAPTER 6

Future Directions

6.1 LANDING IN SHARING ECONOMY

In recent years, a new model has emerged on the market based on the temporary rental of unused goods or the provision of services in order to obtain economic benefits – the sharing economy. Due to the relatively short time and rapid development of this economic model, as well as the lack of corresponding industry regulatory systems and methods, it faces a series of problems. The blockchain's unique data storage mechanism and mode of operation can specifically address some of the current problems in the sharing economy (Hawlitschek, Notheisen, & Teubner, 2018).

6.1.1 Reduce Platform Operating Costs with Decentralised Architecture

The high cost of operation has been a lingering problem in the sharing economy business model, due to the huge investment costs in marketing, post-operation, product maintenance, and other aspects of the enterprise, resulting in the continued decline of many companies' commercial profits, costs continue to rise, and even many companies have gone out of business because of cost issues. For example, bicycle-sharing companies, the production cost of their vehicles ranges from a hundred to a thousand yuan, and after putting them into operation, they are also responsible for maintenance and recycling, which requires a lot of financial and human support, resulting in very high operating costs. Service providers not only need to invest in servers and other infrastructure but also need to be responsible for the normal operation of these servers and invest a lot of human and material resources to ensure the security of business data, which will inevitably lead to high operating costs in the long run. If blockchain technology is used, the original centralised architecture can be removed, so that enterprises no longer need to invest huge amounts of money to build their own server clusters because the data is scattered and stored in different network nodes, each node is only responsible for maintaining the security and accuracy of its own data, and data updates are also broadcasted in the blockchain technology. The chain is released, thus reducing the day-to-day maintenance workload of the company, thus effectively reducing operational costs.

6.1.2 Reduce Single Point of Failure through Distributed Storage Mechanisms

Traditional online systems of sharing economy operators usually use a centralised star-shaped network architecture model, in which the service operator provides services through a single point of a single server cluster, and ordinary users access the corresponding service nodes through the Internet and use the mobile applications provided by the operator to perform various types of business operations. In this model, business processing logic and operational data are stored in a single node, if the core node suffers a malicious attack or data tampering will trigger a single point of failure, so that the entire system immediately goes into a paralyzed state, all users of the client are unable to access services normally, and ultimately, the entire online system cannot function normally. The blockchain has a decentralised feature that can be a good solution to the risk of a single point of failure in the current sharing economy because all the data is scattered and stored in various nodes, the failure of any one node will not affect the normal operation of other nodes, so the introduction of blockchain technology into the traditional sharing economy can effectively avoid a single point of system failure.

6.1.3 Rely on Asymmetric Encryption Algorithm to Protect Users' Private Data

Shared goods in the market operation, over time will accumulate a lot of information related to user, which brings data in many cases involving user privacy issues (Tang et al., 2018). Take the current more popular shared bicycle, for example, the user's daily use data will include information on the user's habits of using the vehicle, the beginning and end of the ride, ride route data, payment records, and bound bank card information, these data are closely related to user privacy. In addition, there are other information closely related to individuals, which are held by the service operators. If improper storage occurs in the process of use, or even if the data is used maliciously by people with ulterior motives, it will bring great security risks to users. Blockchain technology, due to the use of asymmetric encryption and decryption technology, can first encrypt the user's information in the process of use before distributing it to each node for storage, and each node will only record the changing data on the blockchain without access to the specific meaning of the data. Therefore, the use of blockchain technology can maximise the privacy and security of the user.

6.1.4 Use of Data-Storage Sharing Mechanisms to Increase Reuse of Information

At present, China's sharing economy industry is rapidly developing, but due to the rapid development of the market, the establishment of relevant standards is obviously lagging behind, in which the most prominent is the urgent need to establish a standard credit system (Pazaitis, De Filippi, Kostakis, & Change, 2017). The authenticity and accuracy of the credit data collected in this way may have certain problems. It is precisely because the sharing economy has not yet formed a complete and unified credit evaluation system and still remains in the state where different manufacturers are doing things on their own, that credit data standards are not uniform, content is inconsistent, and cannot be shared and used, resulting in the further development of the sharing economy industry being greatly affected. By using blockchain technology, the negative impact of the lack of a credit system can be better resolved. Multiple sharing economy service providers can share the same set of blockchain data, and the credit data generated by users when using the products provided by any service provider can be stored in the same blockchain, thus providing a convenient way for service providers to share user information. Thus, a standard credit system can be easily established by leveraging the technical features of the blockchain.

6.1.5 Using Offline Digital Currency to Shorten the Length of the Money Transmission Chain

As a medium of commodity exchange, money supports the normal operation of the entire economic system, which is also the case in the field of sharing economy. In the real market operation process, the user will usually use a third-party mobile phone payment platform, in the form of electronic money to pay. For example, before a user rents a shared item, the service provider first initiates a one-time payment request from the user, the user uses the payment platform to send a transfer instruction to the bank, requesting that the corresponding amount be transferred from his or her account to the account of the opposite end, and the operator receives bank information confirming the successful operation to provide the user with the corresponding goods rental service (Yi, 2019). It can be seen that although it is only a transaction process, the circulation of currency has gone through a number of complex links, and the frequent circulation of currency among different enterprises and financial institutions has not only increased the length of the currency transmission chain but also increased the process costs. The use of currency blockchain technology can effectively solve the shortcomings of the overly long currency transfer chain. Bitcoin, which has been developing rapidly in recent years, is a good example and worth learning from. The central bank can directly establish a currency blockchain and issue electronic currency based on the blockchain, while the participants in the sharing economy can directly complete the transfer of value through the currency blockchain in each transaction, only need to transfer the digital currency held by themselves to the recipient's name through the blockchain to complete the payment process. The use of blockchain technology to complete the transfer of value can effectively shorten the length of the currency transfer chain and address the additional process costs incurred in the payment process.

Through this new model of multi-blockchain integration with the sharing economy, it can effectively solve a series of problems in the traditional sharing economy field, such as high operating costs, lack of data security protection mechanisms, lack of standard credit system, and inadequate supervision of the industry, and provide good technical support for the healthy development of the sharing economy industries.

6.2 COMBINING WITH CLOUD COMPUTING

Cloud computing is a large-scale, low-cost, web-based computing paradigm designed to provide users with reliable, customisable and secure information technology services. Over the past few years, cloud computing has evolved from a promising business concept to one of the fastest-growing areas of the IT industry (Gai, Guo, Zhu, & Yu, 2020).

As technology continues to evolve, users, while using the computing and storage services provided by cloud computing, are also demanding higher security of data stored in the cloud and reliability of outsourced computing, which is the main obstacle to the further development of cloud computing.

Unlike the traditional computing model where the user has full local control over data computation and storage, cloud computing requires that the user's data and physical servers be centralised and managed by the cloud service provider. The subscriber retains only some control over the leased virtual machines. As a result, users are at risk of having their data integrity, security, and privacy compromised as they are no longer able to monitor and manage their data in real time. To address this situation, a mechanism is needed to remotely protect the security of stored data and data computations, and it must be done in a way that ensures the privacy of users. The de-trusting of blockchain technology, the Merkle hash data structure, and the broader distributed consensus mechanism can be used to address these issues.

The application of blockchain technology to cloud computing, combining the respective advantages of blockchain and cloud computing, builds a remote data integrity verification and secure multi-party computing solution based on blockchain technology (Memon et al., 2020). The solution can solve the problems of data security and computational trust in cloud computing from a technical perspective and apply blockchain technology to cloud computing to provide users with secure and efficient data verification and secure multi-party computing services.

The combination of blockchain and cloud computing skills, from a micro point of view, on the one hand, the use of cloud computing existing root service equipment or according to the actual demand to make corresponding changes to complete the development and application process to speed up, satisfy the future blockchain ecosystem, grass-roots enterprises, academic organisations, open-source organisations, and alliances and financial and other organisations of the blockchain application needs. On the other hand, on cloud computing, 'credible, reliable, controllable' is thought to be that the development of cloud computing will need to go over the 'three mountains', while blockchain skills to decentralisation, anonymity and data cannot be tampered with as the main features, and cloud computing for a long time. The objectives of the exercise are not coincidental (Nayak, Narendra, Shukla, & Kempf, 2018).

In terms of storage, storage within the cloud and storage within the blockchain both consist of common storage media. The difference is that the storage within the cloud computing acts as a resource, often independent of each other, generally using the method of sharing, selected by the application. And the blockchain storage is as the storage space of each node in the chain, the value of the blockchain storage does not lie in the storage itself, but in the block that is linked to each other cannot be changed, is a special storage service, cloud computing does also need such storage service. For example, in combination with the Safe City, data is placed in this type of storage, using immutability, so that video, voice, documents, and so on can be used as a legal basis.

In terms of security, the security in cloud computing is to ensure that the application can be safe, secure, and reliable operation. This security falls under the category of traditional security. The security within the blockchain is to ensure that each data block is not tampered with, the recorded content of the data block is not read by users who do not have a private key. Using this, if you combine cloud computing and secure storage products based on the blockchain, you can plan encrypted storage devices.

6.3 EXPANDING THE VALUE OF ARTIFICIAL INTELLIGENCE

Blockchain and artificial intelligence (AI) are two of the hottest technology trends at the moment. Although these two technologies have highly different developers and applications, researchers have been discussing and exploring their combination. PwC predicts that by 2030, AI will add $15.7 trillion to the world economy, and as a result, global GDP will grow by 14%. According to Gartner's projections, the business value from blockchain technology will increase to $3.1 trillion in the same year (Corea, 2019).

By definition, blockchain is a distributed, decentralised, and immutable ledger for storing encrypted data. AI, on the other hand, is the engine or 'brain' that can analyse and make decisions from the data collected.

It goes without saying that each technology has its own level of complexity, but both AI and blockchain are in a position where they can benefit and help each other.

Since both technologies are capable of influencing and implementing data in different ways, their combination makes sense and can take the use of data to new levels. At the same time, integrating machine learning and

AI into the blockchain, and vice versa, can enhance the infrastructure of the blockchain and improve the potential of AI.

In addition, blockchain can also make AI more coherent and easy to understand, and we can track and determine why decisions are made in machine learning (Wang, Dong, Wang, & Yin, 2019). The blockchain and its ledger can keep track of all the data and variables used to make decisions under machine learning.

In addition, AI can improve the efficiency of the blockchain better than humans can. A look at the way blockchains are currently run on standard computers proves this point, requiring a lot of processing power for even basic tasks.

6.3.1 Intelligent Computing Power

If you want to run the blockchain and all its encrypted data on a computer, you need a lot of processing power. For example, the hash algorithm used to mine Bitcoin takes a hard approach, systematically listing all possible candidates for a solution and checking that each candidate satisfies the problem statement before validating the transaction.

AI offers us an opportunity to get out of this rut and approach the task in a more intelligent and efficient way. Imagine a machine learning-based algorithm that can actually improve its skills in real time if given the proper training data.

6.3.2 Creating Diverse Data Sets

Unlike projects based on AI, blockchain technology creates decentralised, transparent networks that can be accessed by anyone around the world in a blockchain public network environment. While blockchain technology is a ledger of cryptocurrencies, blockchain networks are now being used in many industries to enable decentralisation. For example, SingularityNET is specifically focused on using blockchain technology to encourage a wider distribution of data and algorithms to help ensure the future development of AI and the creation of decentralised AI.

SingularityNET combines blockchain and AI to create a smarter, decentralised AI blockchain network that can host disparate data sets. By creating an application programming interface on the blockchain, it will allow AI agents to communicate with each other. As a result, different algorithms can be built on different data sets.

6.3.3 Data Protection

The development of AI is entirely dependent on the input of data – our data. AI receives information about the world and what is happening in the world through data. Basically, data is the source through which an AI will be able to improve itself (Zhu, Gai, & Li, 2019).

On the other hand, blockchain is essentially a technology that allows for the encrypted storage of data on a distributed ledger. It allows for the creation of completely secure databases that can be viewed by approved parties. When blockchain and AI are combined, we have a backup system for sensitive and high-value personal data.

Medical or financial data is too sensitive to hand over to a company and its algorithms (Huang, Cai, & Zhang, 2009). Storing this data on a blockchain that can be accessed by AI, but only with the permission and through proper procedures, provides us with personalised advice while storing sensitive data securely.

6.3.4 Data Monetisation

Another disruptive innovation that can result from combining these two technologies is data monetisation. Monetising collected data is a huge source of revenue for big companies like Facebook and Google.

Allowing others to decide how to sell data in order to generate profits for the business suggests that data is being commercialised and to our detriment. Blockchain allows us to encrypt and protect our data and use it in any way we see fit. It also allows us to personally monetise our data without compromising our personal information if we wish.

The same applies to AI programs that need our data. In order to learn and develop AI algorithms, AI networks will be required to purchase data directly from their creators through the data marketplace. This would make the whole process much fairer than it is now, and no tech giants would be able to take advantage of its users.

Such a data marketplace would also be open for smaller companies. Developing and providing AI is very expensive for companies that do not generate their own data. Through a decentralised data marketplace, they would be able to access other data that is too expensive and privately held.

6.3.5 Trust in Artificial Intelligence Decision Making

As AI algorithms become smarter through learning, it will become increasingly difficult for data scientists to understand how these programs come to specific conclusions and decisions. This is because AI algorithms will be able to process incredibly large amounts of data and variables. However, we must continue to vet the conclusions that AI draws because we want to make sure that they still reflect reality.

Through the use of blockchain technology, there is an immutable record of all the data, variables, and processes used by the AI in the decision-making process. This makes it much easier to audit the entire process.

With a proper blockchain procedure, all the steps from data input to conclusion can be observed and the observing party will ensure that the data has not been tampered with and it gives credence to the conclusions reached by the AI. This is a necessary step because individuals and companies will not start using AI applications if they do not understand the information that underpins their functionality and decision making.

6.4 PROMOTING THE DEVELOPMENT OF SMART CITIES

The rapid development of Internet information technology, more industries are increasing investment in the industrial Internet. The continuous development of big data, blockchain, AI, and other high-tech, wisdom city was born. However, for wisdom city because of the data carrying capacity, the previous storage method has been unable to meet the underlying architecture required by the wisdom of the city because it does not have the flexibility to expand the storage capacity and cannot store a variety of data at the same time, security issues are also the focus of the wisdom of the city construction, blockchain its decentralised ideas and the need to combine big data, decentralised in a simple way to protect urban security, resulting in urban construction and more stable operation (Ibba, Pinna, Seu, & Pani, 2017).

The application of blockchain technology to big data makes it impossible to modify, add, or delete data on the platform at will, which makes big data extremely flexible, increases storage capacity, and provides both security and technology. The impact of blockchain technology on big data lies in the confirmation of data and data storage, providing a powerful technical complement to the big data platform (Singh, Sharma, Yoon, & Shojafar, 2020). Relying on the integration of big data and blockchain technology, highlighting the value of blockchain technology, making the stored data security and information are both true and convenient for later prediction and analysis. Blockchain is an important and indispensable technology in the era of digital economy.

With the socio-economic development as well as the increase in urban population, cities are facing a variety of pressures, urban management, traffic levels, public services, and other issues, the construction and development of smart cities then emerged (Sharma, Moon & Park, 2017). With the continuous development and maturation of big data, blockchain and other Internet information technology have become an important cornerstone in the construction of smart cities. Smart city contains intelligent transportation, intelligent consumption and intelligent environment and so on many fields, a variety of industries, and blockchain, big data is only a microcosm of Internet technology in the development of science and technology, only give full play to information technology to make the rapid development of urban wisdom to maturity (Chang & Chang, 2018).

In summary, the combination of blockchain technology and AI remain a largely undiscovered area. While the convergence of these two technologies has received considerable academic attention, there are still few projects dedicated to this groundbreaking combination (Pieroni, Scarpato, Di Nunzio, & Fallucchi, 2018).

Combining these two technologies together has the potential to use data in unprecedented ways. Data is a key element in developing and augmenting AI algorithms, and blockchain protects this data by allowing us to audit all the intermediate steps by which AI draws conclusions from the data and allows individuals to monetise the data it generates (Rahman et al., 2019).

AI may be incredibly revolutionary, but it must be designed with extreme care. And blockchain can help with this greatly. How the interplay between the two technologies will develop is anyone's guess, however, its true disruptive potential is clearly there and developing rapidly.

6.5 CHAPTER SUMMARY

Blockchain employs P2P technology, cryptography and consensus algorithms, and has characteristics such as data immutability, collective system maintenance, and open and transparent information. It provides a mechanism for information and value transfer and exchange in an untrustworthy environment and is the cornerstone for building the future value Internet. Through the combination with cloud computing, AI, and other technologies, it has a wide range of application prospects in the sharing economy, smart cities, and other scenarios. In future, the blockchain industry application will accelerate, giving rise to diverse technical solutions, and its performance will be continuously optimised, accelerating the landing from both technology and application directions.

REFERENCES

Chang, S. E., & Chang, C.-Y. (2018). *Application of blockchain technology to smart city service: a case of ridesharing.* 2018 IEEE International Conference on Internet of Things (iThings) and IEEE Green Computing and Communications (GreenCom) and IEEE Cyber, Physical and Social Computing (CPSCom) and IEEE Smart Data (SmartData) (pp. 664–671).

Corea, F. (2019). The convergence of AI and blockchain. In *Applied artificial intelligence: where AI can be used in business* (pp. 19–26). Springer. https://link.springer.com/chapter/10.1007%2F978-3-319-77252-3_4.

Gai, K., Guo, J., Zhu, L., & Yu, S. (2020). Blockchain meets cloud computing: a survey. PP(99), 1.

Hawlitschek, F., Notheisen, B., & Teubner, T. (2018). The limits of trust-free systems: a literature review on blockchain technology and trust in the sharing economy. *Electronic Commerce Research and Applications, 29,* 50–63.

Huang, W.-Y., Cai, Y.-Z., & Zhang, Y. J. N. (2009). Natural phenolic compounds from medicinal herbs and dietary plants: potential use for cancer prevention. *Nutrition and Cancer, 62*(1), 1–20.

Ibba, S., Pinna, A., Seu, M., & Pani, F. E. (2017). *CitySense: blockchain-oriented smart cities.* Proceedings of the XP2017 Scientific Workshops (pp. 1–5). https://dl.acm.org/doi/proceedings/10.1145/3120459.

Memon, R. A., Li, J. P., Ahmed, J., Nazeer, M. I., Ismail, M., & Ali, K. (2020). Cloud-based vs. blockchain-based IoT: a comparative survey and way forward. *Frontiers of Information Technology & Electronic Engineering, 21,* 563–586.

Nayak, S., Narendra, N. C., Shukla, A., & Kempf, J. (2018). *Saranyu: Using smart contracts and blockchain for cloud tenant management.* 2018 IEEE 11th International Conference on Cloud Computing (CLOUD) (pp. 857–861).

Pazaitis, A., De Filippi, P., Kostakis, V., & Change, S. (2017). Blockchain and value systems in the sharing economy: the illustrative case of Backfeed. *Technological Forecasting and Social Change, 125,* 105–115.

Pieroni, A., Scarpato, N., Di Nunzio, L., & Fallucchi, F. (2018). Smarter city: smart energy grid based on blockchain technology. *International Journal on Advanced Science Engineering and Information Technology, 8*(1), 298–306.

Rahman, M. A., Rashid, M. M., Hossain, M. S., Hassanain, E., Alhamid, M. F., & Guizani, M. J. I. A. (2019). Blockchain and IoT-based cognitive edge framework for sharing economy services in a smart city. *IEEE Access 7,* 18611–18621.

Sharma, P. K., Moon, S. Y., & Park, J. H. (2017). Block-VN: a distributed blockchain based vehicular network architecture in smart City. *Journal of Information Processing Systems, 13*(1), 184–195.

Singh, S., Sharma, P. K., Yoon, B., & Shojafar, M. (2020). Convergence of blockchain and artificial intelligence in IoT network for the sustainable smart city. *Sustainable Cities and Society, 63*, 102364.

Tang, Y., Zou, Q., Chen, J., Li, K., Kamhoua, C. A., Kwiat, K., & Njilla, L. (2018). *ChainFS: Blockchain-secured cloud storage.* 2018 IEEE 11th international conference on cloud computing (CLOUD) (pp. 987–990). IEEE.

Wang, K., Dong, J., Wang, Y., & Yin, H. (2019). Securing data with blockchain and AI. IEEE Access. *7*, 77981–77989.

Yi, L. (2019). Optimization mode of sharing economy for data defects based on blockchain. doi:10.12783/dtetr/aemce2019/29517.

Zhu, L., Gai, K., & Li, M. (2019). Blockchain-enabled cloud data preservation services. In *Blockchain Technology in Internet of Things* (pp. 43–52). Springer, Cham. https://doi.org/10.1007/978-3-030-21766-2_4..

Index

Printed in the United States
by Baker & Taylor Publisher Services